Blackness and *mestizaje*
in Mexico and Central America

The Harriet Tubman Series on the African Diaspora

Paul E. Lovejoy and Toyin Falola, eds., *Pawnship, Slavery and Colonialism in Africa*, 2003.

Donald G. Simpson, *Under the North Star: Black Communities in Upper Canada before Confederation (1867)*, 2005.

Paul E. Lovejoy, *Slavery, Commerce and Production in West Africa: Slave Society in the Sokoto Caliphate*, 2005.

José C. Curto and Renée Soulodre-La France, eds., *Africa and the Americas: Interconnections during the Slave Trade*, 2005.

Paul E. Lovejoy, *Ecology and Ethnography of Muslim Trade in West Africa*, 2005.

Naana Opoku-Agyemang, Paul E. Lovejoy and David Trotman, eds., *Africa and Trans-Atlantic Memories: Literary and Aesthetic Manifestations of Diaspora and History*, 2008.

Boubacar Barry, Livio Sansone, and Elisée Soumonni, eds., *Africa, Brazil, and the Construction of Trans-Atlantic Black Identities*, 2008.

Behnaz Asl Mirzai, Ismael Musah Montana, and Paul E. Lovejoy, eds., *Slavery, Islam and Diaspora*, 2009.

Carolyn Brown and Paul E. Lovejoy, eds., *Repercussions of the Atlantic Slave Trade: The Interior of the Bight of Biafra and the African Diaspora*, 2010.

Ute Röschenthaler, *Purchasing Culture in the Cross River Region of Cameroon and Nigeria*, 2011.

Ana Lucia Araujo, Mariana P. Candido and Paul E. Lovejoy, eds., *Crossing Memories: Slavery and African Diaspora*, 2011.

Edmund Abaka, *House of Slaves and "Door of No Return": Gold Coast Castles and Forts of the Atlantic Slave Trade*, 2012.

Christopher Innes, Annabel Rutherford, and Brigitte Bogar, eds. *Carnival: Theory and Practice*, 2012.

Paul E. Lovejoy and Benjamin P. Bowser, *The Transatlantic Slave Trade and Slavery*, 2012.

Dorsía Smith Silva and Simone A. James Alexander, *Feminist and Critical Perspectives on Caribbean Mothering*, 2013.

Hakim Adi, *Pan-Africanism and Communism: The Communist International, Africa and the Diaspora, 1919-1939*, 2013.

Elisabeth Cunin and Odile Hoffmann, *Blackness and Mestizaje in Mexico and Central America*, 2013.

Harriet Tubman Series

Blackness and *Mestizaje*
in Mexico and Central America

Edited by

Elisabeth Cunin
and Odile Hoffmann

AFRICA WORLD PRESS

TRENTON | LONDON | CAPE TOWN | NAIROBI | ADDIS ABABA | ASMARA | IBADAN | NEW DELHI

AFRICA WORLD PRESS
541 West Ingham Avenue | Suite B
Trenton, New Jersey 08638

Book and Cover design: Saverance Publishing Services
Cover photo: Manuel González de la Parra

Library of Congress Cataloging-in-Publication Data

Blackness and mestizaje in Mexico and Central America / edited by Elisabeth Cunin and Odile Hoffmann.
    pages cm
    Includes bibliographical references and index.
    ISBN 978-1-59221-932-2 (hard cover) -- ISBN 978-1-59221-933-9 (paperback) 1. Blacks--Race identity--Mexico. 2. Blacks--Race identity--Central America. 3. Mestizaje--Mexico. 4. Mestizaje--Central America. 5. Multiculturalism--Mexico. 6. Multiculturalism--Central America. 7. Mexico--Race relations. 8. Central America--Race relations. I. Cunin, Elisabeth, 1971- II. Hoffmann, Odile.
    F1392.B55B56 2013
    305.800972--dc23
                        2013000812

The Harriet Tubman Institute for Research on the Global Migrations of African Peoples

Table of Contents

Tables

$\mathcal{A}$cknowledgements

This book offers a sample of a larger work, which consists of four volumes published in Mexico in 2010-2011, dedicated to people of African descent and their roles and places in Latin American societies of yesterday and today. It is a collective effort undertaken within the framework of two international research programs, AFRODESC "People of African Descent and Slaveries: Domination, Identification and Heritages in the Americas (15th - 21st centuries)" (ANR-Suds AIRD AFRODESC 07-SUDS-008) and EURESCL-WP4 "Slave Trade, Slavery, Abolitions and their Legacies in European Histories and Identities" (7th PCRD European Program) and involving several institutions, including CEMCA, CIESAS, INAH and UNAM in Mexico; and the IRD, the University of Paris Diderot and the University of Nice in France.

These books are the result of a dialogue between scientists from Mexico, Central America, Europe, and North America in the Congress, "Diaspora, nation and difference. Populations of African origin in Mexico and Central America," held in Veracruz, Mexico, in 2008. The event proposed contextualized and politicized interpretations of the "black question" in the region and laid the foundations for a theoretical, methodological, political and ethical renewal in order to understand the ethnic and cultural diversity of Latin American societies and the difficulties they face to confront persistent inequality and racism.

We decided to include another text devoted to Afro-Mexican studies although it was published in other languages some years ago (Hoffmann 2005, 2006), since the broad lines of analysis and the contributions remain valid.

MÉXICO, ELISABETH CUNIN AND ODILE HOFFMANN

Introduction

Elisabeth Cunin and Odile Hoffmann

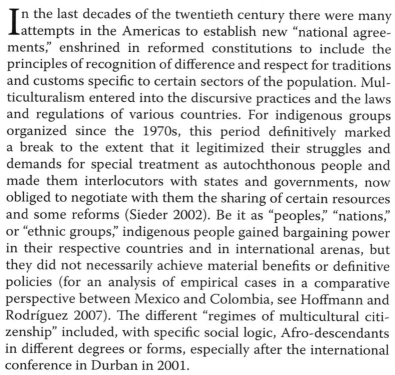

In the last decades of the twentieth century there were many attempts in the Americas to establish new "national agreements," enshrined in reformed constitutions to include the principles of recognition of difference and respect for traditions and customs specific to certain sectors of the population. Multiculturalism entered into the discursive practices and the laws and regulations of various countries. For indigenous groups organized since the 1970s, this period definitively marked a break to the extent that it legitimized their struggles and demands for special treatment as autochthonous people and made them interlocutors with states and governments, now obliged to negotiate with them the sharing of certain resources and some reforms (Sieder 2002). Be it as "peoples," "nations," or "ethnic groups," indigenous people gained bargaining power in their respective countries and in international arenas, but they did not necessarily achieve material benefits or definitive policies (for an analysis of empirical cases in a comparative perspective between Mexico and Colombia, see Hoffmann and Rodríguez 2007). The different "regimes of multicultural citizenship" included, with specific social logic, Afro-descendants in different degrees or forms, especially after the international conference in Durban in 2001.

Indeed, in the same period and in articulation with the indigenous sector, the black movement began to emerge as a visible force in Latin America. However, unlike the earlier indigenous movements, it did not enjoy a legitimizing discourse in the international arena as an "autochthonous" or "indigenous" group. It began to grow, then, in a very disperse form around localized demonstrations based as appropriate on the fight against discrimination and racism, cultural claims, demands for land or access to health and education, among others. The diversity of action largely reflects the wide range of situations in the places inhabited by African descendants in America, which Juliet Hooker (2010, 46-47) organized into four main "types": the "afro-mestizos," descendants of colonial slaves and mixed in the societies for several centuries, and who have not developed specific collective identities; those who are also descendants of colonial slaves, but who have developed racialized identities, as in Brazil; the descendants or members of communities of escaped slaves, like the Garifuna; and finally the West Indians of African descent who arrived in Central America in the ninetieth and twentieth centuries, mostly as migrant workers in plantations or on the railroad.

We do not wish to delve into this typology and its relevance, but rather to stress that this variety shows that it is neither possible nor desirable to seek a unique pattern relative to black populations, not even that which is based on diversity, hybridity, fluidity, and mobility united around the concept of "Diaspora" in the works of Appadurai (1996), Gilroy (1993) or Chivallon (2004), particularly in the case of Latin America (Cunin 2009).

As for public policies of difference related to populations of African descent, we also recognize several lines developed from the 1990s. Two countries have been the subjects of multiple investigations because of the magnitude of the changes introduced: Colombia and Brazil. In Colombia the "multicultural revolution" of the 1990s has been studied, based on a definition of multiculturalism that is pragmatic but accepted, concrete, regulated and effective, even if partially, and that recognizes territorial, political, and social rights of Afro-descendants, considered as an "ethnic group." In Brazil, studies have shown that, on the one hand, there is recognition of the territorial claims of the Quilombolas, yet on the other hand a model of quotas is adopted to regulate differential access to educational, health, and other resources on a phenotypic and explicitly racialized basis. More recently, other Latin American countries have begun to develop their own measures, using these two models (Ecuador), introducing more radical changes (Bolivia), or simply acknowledging cultural rights or promoting research (Argentina).

How are Mexico and Central America located in this range of positions and orientations? In Mexico the interpretive models, developed since the 1950s and especially in the 1980s around the idea of a "third root," described the populations of African descent as a "historical fact," a group that was the carrier of certain "cultural traits," but that until a few years ago had no political presence (Hoffmann in this volume). Indeed, they were denied any sociological relevance, which led the African militants to consider themselves the "missing link" of America in the great concert of Afro-Latinos, a population that would suffer from a lack of identity or, worse, that would deny its origins and identities. In Central America the story is different, not only because of the demographic importance of Afro-descendants that came with colonization and trade (the so-called "black colonials") but also because of the presence of the Garifuna, and French and British West Indians (Barrow and Priestley 2003, Euraque 2004, Hooker 2005, Amaya 2007, Anderson 2007). However, there are few countries that have implemented specific measures, despite legislative initiatives in this direction in Guatemala, Nicaragua, and Honduras in the 1980s and 1990s. This region allows us to deepen the relationship between nation and the role of peoples of African descent, as it is marked by the complex dynamics of nation building intersecting with regional divisions (the "enclave" of the Atlantic coast) and transnational forces (political movements, plantation economy, and social movements).

This book argues that people of African descent in Mexico and Central America do not suffer from "identity deficit" but rather they do not fit into the "classical" interpretations and are therefore not easily categorized in known analytical schemes. By the same token they have much to teach us, and their analysis has to be located at the intersection of ethnic and political perspectives, *mestizaje* ideology, and cultural viewpoints. Mexican

and Central American configurations, because of their original-
ity, force us to adopt plural visions, and not always from the
binomial dominant-dominated, but also toward the margins,
the edges, the borders, with particular emphasis on situations of
mixtures and ambiguous categories (Afro-indigenous, creoles,
mestizos), multiple belongings (national and transnational), or
seemingly contradictory practices (black music and religion
without black people, mobilization without ethnic claims). We
will rely on the collective work of D. Euraque, J. L. Gould, and C.
Hale (2004) on Central America, returning to their idea of continuity between *mestizaje* and multiculturalism, as ideologies of
government for the management of differences. This concept
leads us to propose that, beyond the ideal of a homogenized
citizenship produced by *mestizaje*, there are complex dynamics
of claims based on difference and indifference, stigmatization
and fascination (Lhamon 1998), homogenization and othering.
In this regard, we believe that *mestizaje* is not only a "myth"
and multiculturalism a "challenge" to it, and that we have to
further investigate the different processes of racialization, ethnicization, and negotiation of the belongings that characterize
mestizaje as multiculturalism.

This begins to depict what might be some specificities
of the political projects for African groups and collectives in
Central America and Mexico: their necessary renouncement to
unambiguous explanations. Using the debates on the respective weights of agency and structure, political actors and institutions, transnational networks and initiatives rooted in local
areas, the state and grassroots organizations, the essays in this
book go beyond simple proposals and hope to assert and prove
the political dimension of the negotiations of rural and urban
communities and collectives of Afro-descendants with their
respective environments.

The scenes of everyday life are analyzed by Miguel
Gonzalez, who studies the interactions and tensions between
ethnic groups of the Atlantic Coast of Nicaragua, within the
framework of the regional autonomy system (RAAN and

RAAS, Autonomous Regions of the North and South Atlantic) granted by the Sandinista government after violent conflicts. In a context of the recognition of limited multicultural citizenship, the struggle for the legitimacy of their rights brought forward groups and collectives who all demand more democracy and greater autonomy, but who do not always converge in their methods and resources. This leads the author to discuss the alleged positive correlation between democracy and autonomy in the autonomous regime. For blacks and indigenous peoples of the Atlantic coast of Nicaragua, according to Gonzalez, the regional autonomy regime is in fact a "restricted inclusion" to national citizenship, which certainly creates new opportunities for participation but, at the same time, fails to resolve tensions between sectors. One could follow this line and ask what happens to the mestizos that reside in the same regions of the Atlantic but are not part of the multicultural scheme proposed by the autonomy regimes. Might one introduce the notion of "imposed inclusion" to account for this regime that seeks to include on the basis of a partition into groups, and therefore excludes those who do not belong to them? Another key aspect of the political struggle has to do with the negotiation of the specific spaces in which it develops, that is, the issue of the districts where the autonomy regime is applied, which are at the same time the spaces where the debates, the contradictions, the tensions and the conflicts of everyday life are constructed. Far from being a technical or administrative issue, the delimitation of community, political and electoral entities or units refers to certain concepts about the group, its cohesion and diversity: Who should be a neighbor of whom? Who decides where the line should go?

Elisabeth Cunin shows how, in the case of Belize, ethnic identity is at once both denied and used by political actors in the early years of independence in the 1980s. From a "multicultural" model—before its time—associated with British colonialism, succeeds an effort to build a "creole nation" that will lead to a kind of "ethnic war," also not named or declared, which seems to lead to an accelerated process of ethnicization of all the socio-cultural components of the country, starting with the Creoles. Without articulating it and thus escaping the models implemented in other countries, Belize constructs its recent national history in the midst of contradictions and of very original theoretical and political innovations.

Carlos Agudelo is interested in the complex web of organizations, groups, and sectors of the black movement in Central America. This allows him to highlight the role of international bodies and to show how militant networks are established with a certain hierarchy and based on the control of resources, both material (trips, allowances) and intangible (knowledge, discourses, prestige). In these networks, which are rarely horizontal, a clientelistic logic is articulated with vicissitudes and contingencies, personal affinities and opportunities that enable or hinder cooperation between groups. In the precarious conditions of daily life of the militants, the priorities are negotiated on a permanent basis and the construction of common ideological discourses becomes difficult if not impossible and undesirable.

Starting the series of works on Mexico, Odile Hoffmann proposes a review of viewpoints and approaches that have historically dealt with the issue. She gives a critical account of "Afro-Mexican" studies (antecedents, currents) and proposes an analytical framework for understanding the specificities of the Mexican case. Through the study of certain cultural institutions and certain actors (activists, intellectuals) she analyses the ambiguities of the ethnicization of the black population, which, although located in part in the regional context of affirmation of multiculturalism, refers mostly to the specific dynamics of the construction of the colony and later of the Mexican nation. Going beyond the reference to the "third root," the article is a call to investigate the flexibility and permeability of group boundaries, the unstable and unfinished processes of identification.

Gloria Lara examines the emergence of the ethno-political reference in Mexico, more precisely in the Costa Chica of Oaxaca and Guerrero. Based on long and intense fieldwork, she describes how a "black current" is being constructed since the 1990s; she reconstructs their genealogy and their internal diversity. This allows her to escape from two hazards: one that tends to undervalue the black mobilization in Mexico, citing its "inauthenticity" because of its very recent nature and weak local acceptance, and another that on the contrary overestimates the role and impact of Afro-descendant organizations, groups that only bring together a few dozen individuals, sometimes much less. Whatever its importance, the existence and dynamics of this movement can no longer be denied and thus deserves analytical attention.

Christian Rinaudo deconstructs the association "Veracruz-black" and shows that it is a result of historical and touristic discourses and public policies. He presents a critical approach to the analyses in terms of "ethnic groups," which emphasizes the processes of categorization and social uses of the categories, rather than the "groups" or "populations," and thus opens novel approaches based on notions such as "ethnicity without ethnic groups" (Brubaker 2002) or "blackness without ethnicity." (Sansone 2003) According to Rinaudo, the several instances of *mestizaje*, not just ideological but "real," force us to abandon the study of "black people" in favor of an approach in terms of social processes of distinction between "black" and "not black." He presents within this logic an ethnography of Veracruz, which emphasizes "the contexts or the moments" more than the groups, and he explores various avenues of research, which tend to set a true work program.

Finally Nahayeilli Juárez shows an interest in *santería*, addressed in an original way: not as an "African religion" which would lead one to study the elements of survival, but as a part of contemporary processes of transnationalization, between Cuba and Mexico mainly, with ramifications in the US and Africa. Juárez discusses *santería* as a symbol of African-American culture that travels around, and its relocation in Mexico City in the years 1940-50, linked to the music, film and entertainment industries. *Santería* in Mexico is associated with both blacks and non-blacks; it is confused with other practices not ethnically or racially marked (Catholicism, popular cultures). Thus appear "Afro signs" that circulate among various territories and that do not mechanically produce "an African identity."

Notes

1. Hoffmann, Odile coord. 2010. *Política e identidad. Afrodescendientes en México y América Central.* México: INAH-UNAM-CEMCA-IRD; Cunin, Elisabeth coord. 2010. *Mestizaje, diferencia y nación. "Lo negro" en América Central y el Caribe.* México: INAH-UNAM-CEMCA-IRD; de la Serna, Juan Manuel, coord. 2010. *De la libertad y la abolición: Africanos y afrodescendientes en Iberoamérica.* México: INAH-UNAM-CEMCA-IRD; Velázquez, María Elisa coord. 2011. *Debates históricos contemporáneos: africanos y afrodescendientes de México y Centroamérica.* México: INAH-UNAM-CEMCA-IRD.

2. Editorial norms in relation to proper names are always subject to debate. In this case, and following the preferences of Garifuna authors, we chose to use "Garifuna" invariably, without a plural form.

Bibliography

Aguirre Beltrán, Gonzalo. 1984 [1946]. *La población negra de México.* México: Fondo de Cultura Económica.

Amaya, Jorge Alberto. 2007. *Las imágenes de los negros Garífunas en la literatura hondureña y extranjera.* Honduras: Secretaría de Cultura, Artes y Deportes.

Anderson, Mark. 2007. When Afro Becomes (Like) Indigenous: Garífuna and Afro-Indigenous Politics in Honduras. *Journal of Latin American and Caribbean Anthropology* 12(2): 384-413.

Appadurai, Arjun. 1996. *Modernity at Large. Cultural Dimensions of Globalisation.* Minneapolis: University of Minnesota Press.

Barrow, Alberto and George Priestley. 2003. *Piel oscura Panamá: reflexiones al filo del Centenario.* Panamá: Universal Books.

Brubaker, Rogers. 2002. Ethnicity without Groups. *Archives Européennes de Sociologie* 43(2): 163-189.

Castellanos, Alicia, ed. 2008. *Racismo e Identidades. Sudáfrica y Afrodescendientes en las Américas.* México: División de Ciencias Sociales y Humanidades, UAM-Iztapalapa.

Chivallon, Cristine. 2004. *La diaspora noire des Amériques. Expériences et théories à partir de la Caraïbe.* Paris: CNRS Editions.

Cunin, Elisabeth. 2009. Des 'Amériques noires' à la 'Black Atlantic' : réflexions sur la diaspora à partir de l'Amérique latine. In *Autour de 'l'Atlantique noir'. Une polyphonie de perspectives*, eds. Carlos Agudelo, Capucine Boidin, Livio Sansone. Paris: IHEAL.

Euraque, Darío. 2004. *Conversaciones históricas con el mestizaje y su identidad nacional en Honduras*. Honduras: Centro Editorial.

Euraque, Dario, Jeffrey L. Gould and Charles Hale. 2004. *Memorias del Mestizaje. Cultura política en Centroamérica de 1920 al presente*. Guatemala: CIRMA.

Gilroy, Paul. 1993. *The Black Atlantic. Modernity and Double Consciousness*. Londres: Verso.

Hall, Stuart. 1994 [1990]. Cultural identity and diaspora. *Anthro 251. Issues on Cultural Studies*, Stanford Bookstore 222-237.

Hoffmann, Odile and María Teresa Rodríguez. 2007. *Retos de la diferencia. Los actores de la multiculturalidad entre México y Colombia*. México: CEMCA, CIESAS, IRD.

Hooker, Juliet. 2005. Indigenous Inclusion/ Black Exclusion: Race, Ethnicity and Multicultural Citizenship in Latin America. *Journal of Latin American Studies* 37(2): 285-310.

Hooker, Juliet. 2010. Las luchas por los derechos colectivos de los afrodescendientes en América Latina. In *Política e identidad. Afrodescendientes en México y América Central*, ed. Odile Hoffmann, 31-64. México: INAH-UNAM-CEMCA-IRD.

Lhamon, William T. Junior. 1998. *Raising Cain. Blackface performance from Jim Crow to Hip-Hop*. Harvard University Press.

Sansone, Livio. 2003. *Blackness without ethnicity. Constructing race in Brazil*. New York: Palgrave Macmillan.

Sieder, Rachel. 2002. *Multiculturalism in Latin America. Indigenous Rights, Diversity and Democracy*. London: Palgrave Macmillan, Institut of Latin American Studies.

Chapter 1

Indigenous, Afro-Descendant, and Mestizo Costeños: Limited Inclusion in the Autonomy Regime of Nicaragua[1]

Miguel González

———————— ⚭ ————————

This chapter discusses the historical origins, legal framework, and development of the multiethnic autonomous regime established at the beginning of the 1990s on the Atlantic Caribbean Coast of Nicaragua. The autonomy process as it has unfolded in the region has served as an important political and legal model for the inclusion of ethnic and cultural diversity, not only in Nicaragua, but also in the wider Latin American context as a whole. In the chapter, I devote some attention to the inclusion of the Coast's Afro-descendant population (Garifuna and Creoles), but I also present general features about the participation of indigenous peoples (Miskitu, Sumu-Mayangna, and Rama) and the mestizo communities.

The study investigates the perspectives of the different members of *costeño* (coastal) society with respect to their rights of representation, in ethnic and racial terms, and examines the forms of activism and political alliances they have constructed to achieve such representation. I argue that a new cycle is being initiated among the Nicaraguan costeño communities as they continue their struggle to consolidate their multicultural citizenship rights (which include both individual and collective rights) in the context of the autonomy regime.

Political community and the autonomous subject

In some studies in the theoretical literature regarding autonomy regimes in Latin America, various assumptions have been established that are rarely supported in empirical studies. I concentrate on two of these assumptions: 1) that in order to advance, autonomy requires the constitution of an autonomous "ethnic" subject (López y Rivas 1995, López Barcenas 2007); and 2) that there exists a mutual and enriching relationship between autonomy and democracy (Díaz-Polanco and Sánchez 2002). My aim is to demonstrate that these assumptions do not contribute sufficiently to our ability to understand the complex dynamic of the interrelationships between and among the indigenous peoples and ethnic groups in the autonomy regime on the Nicaraguan Atlantic Caribbean Coast.

The autonomous "ethnic" subject is a rather mysterious if not confusing formulation. Some authors have used it in order to represent ethnic social actors that have mobilized for the defense of their rights in the context of autonomous regimes. Gilberto López y Rivas, for example, tells us that in order to operate effectively autonomy and self-government require:

> The conformation of an autonomous subject with a territorial base and a socio-ethnic identity that represents, by consensus, the interests of the communities comprising the autonomous region in such a way that it emerges as a recognized interlocutor toward the national government for negotiating capacities and powers. (López y Rivas 1995, 30. My translation)

This author also indicates that, "the autonomous subject has to assume the heterogeneity of the ethnic regions in his/her socio-ethnic composition" (López y Rivas 1995, 31). It would seem that here the autonomous "ethnic" subject would be the distinct organized groups acting through autonomous political institutions.

In the same vein, Díaz-Polanco underlines the importance of a "political collective" or collective subject that emerges as the entity that galvanizes the struggle for autonomy (Díaz-Polanco 1997, 153). But here arise a series of questions: How is this collectivity formed? What are the conditions of its formation or non-formation? How can we deal with the heterogeneities (of class, race, and gender) that are characteristic of the diverse people and communities that inhabit autonomous regions and territories? In the past, what has been the nature of the interactions between people and the political institutions that have resulted from the creation of autonomous governments? What is the nature of these interactions today? How do these dynamics relate to the collective aspiration constitutive of autonomy?

In what they refer to as the relation between autonomy and democracy, Díaz-Polanco and Sánchez consider that:

> ...democratic and autonomist ideals have in common an interest in self-government, participation, and the development of socio-cultural plurality, as well as the search for the decentralization and devolution of powers and authorities, congregated in the central state and its apparatus toward collective entities or territories and their members. (Díaz-Polanco and Sánchez 2002, 43. My translation)

From my perspective, it is not enough to enunciate a supposed positive synergy between democracy and autonomy without first problematizing the concrete interaction that is constructed in the life of autonomous regimes. As I hope to demonstrate, ideals of multicultural coexistence are mediated in a concrete manner by regimes of rights, mechanisms of political representation, and the social participation that regional autonomy is capable of establishing and promoting among the groups for whom autonomy has been granted.

Other literature has recently explored the question of what can be called an "interior space" of political territorial autonomy. For example, Weller and Wolff (2005), editors of a collection of essays about different experiences of autonomy, have noted that territorial autonomy has a dual character: "i) providing devolved government to the entire resident population within a given territory irrespective of ethnicity and also ii) increasing the level of self-governance for a particular ethnic group within this territory" (2005, 268). These authors also suggest that "regardless of the degree of autonomy granted to the specific territory, the country's overall constitutional framework will be preserved" (Wolff and Weller 2005, 14). In sum, in order to function well, autonomy demands the sharing of power.

With respect to the theme of governability, Wolff and Weller state that "autonomy regulations need to provide for social-structural conditions that ensure the necessary degree of political homogeneity, an institutional consensus about the political process in the autonomous area in which all ethnic groups living there have a stake," while the same time, "affording each ethnic group enough independence to address the specific concerns of its own members within an overall framework that includes mechanisms for dispute resolution in cases where accommodating one group's concerns has the potential to disadvantage unduly another group" (2005, 16). The authors emphasize that "territorial autonomy regulations alone are very unlikely" to achieve these things and that additional mechanisms are necessary to reinforce a sense of inclusion and cohesion, starting with appropriate balances that guarantee the rights and interests of the groups (2005, 16).

In sum, these reflections help us to understand that the political collectivity needs to ensure a level of social integration in existing autonomy regimes that recognizes the heterogeneity and different views of distinct groups. They also help us to question the extent to which the institutional framework guarantees the effective exercise of individual and collective rights. In this manner, a better interpretation can emerge about how to define the term autonomous "ethnic" subject as a collective entity. In other words, we can see if autonomy has meant, effectively, a major inclusion of diversity and a better democracy. If so, we can ask, what type of democracy and what type of autonomy?

Following from the above, my aim is to problematize and at the same time explore the distinctly contentious perspectives that elucidate the present development of the autonomy regime on the Atlantic Coast of Nicaragua. The process toward the construction of legitimacy within a framework of multicultural citizenship rights presents a very interesting scenario for exploring the intersections, possible convergences, and tensions in the relations between indigenous costeño people (Miskitu, Rama, and Sumu-Mayangna) and non-indigenous costeño people (Afro-descendant Garifuna and Creoles and costeño mestizos).[2]

Population, autonomy, institutions, and political participation

The population of the Nicaraguan Atlantic Caribbean Coast constitutes a multicultural, heterogeneous society. It is comprised of three population groups: 1) indigenous peoples (Sumu-Mayangna, Rama, and Miskitu); 2) people of African descent (Garifuna and Creole); and 3) costeño mestizos. In the 1982 census, the total population was estimated at 282 thousand inhabitants with a breakdown as follows: 64.6% mestizo, 23.7% Miskitu, 9.1% Creole, 1.72% Sumu, 0.53% Caribs (or Garifuna), and 0.23% Rama (CIDCA, 1982: 49). According to the most recent census of 2005, the Coast's total population was approximately 620 100 inhabitants (*Gobierno de Nicaragua*, 2006). Of this number, mestizos constituted approximately 76% and Miskitu formed 17%. These two groups were followed by Creole with 3.6%, Sumu-Mayangna with 2.6%, and finally Garifuna and Rama with 0.55% and 0.175%, respectively.

The ethno-cultural composition of the overall population has varied historically, but in the last two decades diverse factors such as the *contra* war against the former Sandinista revolutionary government (1979-1990) and various economic changes in the country have led to a major redistribution of the original population throughout the coastal region. Meanwhile, state policies and poverty have caused an increase in the mestizo population on the Coast due to the ongoing in-migration of mestizos from the western side or Pacific region of the country. The rate of annual increase of the populations of the North and South Autonomous Atlantic Coast regions is around 4% above that of the national rate.[3]

During the 1980s, shortly following the revolutionary triumph in 1979 of the FSLN (Sandinista National Liberation Front), the Coast experienced an armed conflict of great magnitude. Owing to initial errors of the FSLN government in its politics toward the Coast, the costeño population (the indigenous and Afro-descendant groups in particular) reacted, demanding a series of rights. These rights focused on the theme of collective ownership of indigenous land and control of natural resources, social and political participation, and the protection of ethnocultural identity. Underlying the conflict between the Coast and the Nicaraguan state was a period of more than three centuries of mutual distrust in the relationship between "Pacific" or "Spanish" Nicaragua and the "Atlantic" or "Caribbean" Coast which had had a long history of influence from, first, Britain and, later, the North American enclave economy. It is necessary to emphasize that the historical and cultural tensions between both the eastern and western Nicaraguan societies were also intensified by the confrontation that the United States government staged against the emerging revolutionary government under the FSLN.[4]

The contra war was clearly a divisive social process. However, it was also to become a moment of recognition between the two Nicaraguas. Eventually, there was a better understanding on the part of the Nicaraguan state toward the demands of the indigenous and Afro-descendant populations on the Coast that had been opposed to the Revolution. In 1987, as an indication of that understanding, the FSLN government approved the Autonomy Statute for "the communities of the Coast," establishing a multicultural citizenship regime for costeño inhabitants (Asamblea Nacional de Nicaragua 1987).

The Autonomy Statute recognizes a series of cultural, social, and political rights for the population of the Atlantic Coast. Among these are the right to enjoy and benefit from the region's natural resources, the right to maintain traditional forms of organization, the right to collective ownership of land, and the right to bilingual education (Asamblea Nacional de Nicaragua 1987). The Statute does not make a distinction between the recognized rights of Afro-descendants and indigenous peoples. Basically, both groups enjoy the same rights. However, the Statute is somewhat general and ambiguous, leaving substantial questions (for example, questions of land and the exploitation of natural resources, and those of relations between autonomous institutions and the state) without clear procedures or an enabling legislation (Frühling et al. 2007).

In a study of the types of demands articulated on the part of Miskitu and Creole groups at the moment of the formation of the Autonomy Statute, Gabbert (2006) has noted that the Miskitu perceived that ethnic and territorial autonomy would confer a predominant role on their particular group. Meanwhile, the Creole perceived a vision of multiethnic, regional self-government, inclusive of other groups, including the mestizos. Gabbert explains these differences in perception according to distinct structural conditions (level of integration and internal social differentiation) that exist between Miskitus and Creoles. According to him, the Miskitu can be characterized as an "*ethnie*," while Creoles are more clearly an "ethnic group."[5] For Gabbert, these differences imply distinct political potentialities and political visions of autonomy for each group. In the end, the Autonomy Statute put an emphasis on a model of multiethnic regional representation, marginalizing ethnic-specific autonomy, territorial autonomy, and indigenous autonomy in particular.[6]

The Statute also established two autonomous regional councils—one in the North Atlantic Autonomous Region or RAAN and situated in the port town of Bilwi, and the other in the South Atlantic Autonomous Region or RAAS and situated in the port city of Bluefields. The councils are made up of forty-five members, are elected by universal suffrage every four years, and represent each of the ethnic groups and indigenous peoples living in the regions.[7] The councils are governing and legislative organs and they deliberate upon regional interests as the "superior authorities" of each autonomous region. Among the councils' powers are the following: 1) to participate in the elaboration, planning, implementation, and follow-up of the political, economic, social, and cultural programs that affect or concern the region; 2) to resolve boundary disputes within the different communities according to their respective territory; 3) to elaborate a system of taxation for the region; 4) to monitor the correct utilization of the special fund for the development and social promotion of the region that will be established with regard to internal and external resources and other supplemental funds; and 5) to elect among their members a Regional Coordinator and members of the Directive Board of the council.

The Statute, moreover, also stipulates that communal land cannot be embargoed, alienated, or subjected to prescription. That is, communal land cannot be sold or used as collateral for loans. These rights do not extinguish as contemplated in the Autonomy Statute and the National Constitution. As well, the Statute recognizes the right of the communities as beneficiaries of the usufruct of the natural resources located in the territories of the Coast (Asamblea Nacional de Nicaragua 1987).

Upon their election, the two regional councils established special electoral districts in the two autonomous regions and, in addition, they fixed criteria for ethnic representation. The system of political representation assured that members of the distinct ethnic groups could succeed at being elected to the councils by means of closed slates for regional and national political parties.[8] In this way, Miskitus, Sumu-Mayangnas, Ramas, Garifuna, Creoles, and mestizos obtain formal representation in the multiethnic regional councils. The first autonomous regional councils were elected in 1990. To date, there have been six successive councils elected.

What has ethnic representation been like in the councils since their establishment and how is this diversity expressed in autonomous representation? Tables 1 and 2 are illustrative:

Table 1.1. North Atlantic Autonomous Region (RAAN): Political and Ethnic Distribution of Seats Regional Autonomous Council, 1990 - 2014[9]

ETHNIC GROUP	POLITICAL ORGANIZATION					% OF REPRESENTATION IN THE REGIONAL COUNCIL	% REGIONAL POPULATION
	FSLN	PLC	UNO	YATAMA	PAMUC		
Mestizos	63	64	3	0	0	45	56.7
Miskitu	33	24	0	71	1	45	36.2
Creole	10	2	0	4	0	5.6	1.2
Mayangna	8	4	0	1	0	4.5	5.9
Sub-total	**114**	**94**	**3**	**76**	**1**	100%	100%

FSLN (Frente Sandinista de Liberacion Nacional); PLC (Partido Liberal Constitucionalista); UNO (Unión Nacional Opositora); YATAMA (Yapti Tasba Masrika Nanih Asla Takanka); PAMUC (Partido Movimiento de Unidad Costeña)[10]

From these figures, we can deduce that in the RAAN: 1) the national parties (the PLC and FSLN) prefer mestizos as councilors, above the other ethnic groups; 2) mestizos and Miskitu achieve most representation, particularly with regard to the PLC and FSLN; 3) with respect to other political organizations, the FSLN is relatively more inclusive of ethnic diversity; 4) YATAMA has been consolidated as a party representing Miskitus; and 5) Creoles and Sumu-Mayangnas are minority groups in the composition of the RAAN council, besides constituting an important part of the regional population. It is notable that, in the case of the Creoles, a major degree of representation has been reached relative to their demographic weight, a situation that contrasts with the Sumu-Mayangna.

Table 1.2. South Atlantic Autonomous Region (RAAS): Political and
Ethnic Distribution of Seats Regional Autonomous Council, 1990 - 2010[11]

ETHNIC GROUP	POLITICAL ORGANIZATION					% OF REPRESENTATION IN THE REGIONAL COUNCIL	% REGIONAL POPULATION
	FSLN	PLC	UNO	YATAMA	PAMUC		
Mestizos	47	87	10	0	4	52	88.6
Miskitu	3	4	2	13	1	9.2	3.7
Creole	24	16	12	9	8	23	6.08
Mayangna	4	3	1	3	1	4.3	0.28
Garifuna	6	7	2	0	1	5.7	1.02
Rama	5	6	1	0	2	5	0.32
Sub-total	**89**	**123**	**28**	**25**	**17**	**100%**	**100%**

From these figures, we can deduce that in the RAAS: 1) the national parties, especially the PLC, prefer mestizos as councilors, following a pattern relative to the weight of the mestizo population; 2) mestizos and Creoles have achieved major representation (particularly with respect to the PLC, FSLN, and UNO, all of which are national parties) and Creoles in particular have obtained major representation relative to their population weight; meanwhile it can be argued that mestizos appear underrepresented; 3) the FSLN is relatively more inclusive of ethnic diversity; 4) YATAMA is a party of Miskitu and Creole representatives; and 5) Miskitus, Ramas, and Garifuna are minorities in the composition of the RAAS council, as they are in the regional demographic composition.

Hodgson (2004), moreover, has noted how changes in the demographic composition of several electoral districts have resulted in incongruencies with respect to the electoral procedures of indigenous and Afro-descended peoples. In at least six of the ten districts in which the list of candidates should be headed by members of a determined ethnic group, the majority of voters belong to a distinct ethnic group. This situation has important implications for forms of political representation. [12]

Regarding gender, the participation of women in the regional councils in general has been limited. Since 1990, and following six regional elections, women have occupied only 16 per cent of electoral seats in the regional council of the RAAN (see Table 1.3). In the case of the RAAS, the figure is a little higher at 18.4 per cent. Figueroa (2006) has noted that the system of representation in the regional councils discriminates against women, at times reproducing the logic of ethnic discrimination. From Tables 1.3 and 1.4 we can infer, for example, that Sumu-Mayangna women have fewer possibilities of being elected to the autonomous regional councils. In the RAAS, this pattern of exclusion is expressed with respect to Miskitu and Rama women, as can be observed in Table 1.4.

Table 1.3. North Atlantic Autonomous Region (RAAN): Elected women, ethnicity, and political parties, 1990-2014

ETHNIC GROUP	POLITICAL ORGANIZATION			TOTAL
	FSLN	PLC	YATAMA	
Miskitu	6	2	12	20
Mestizo	10	7	0	17
Sumu-Mayangna	1	0	0	1
Creole	6	1	1	8
Sub-total	23	10	13	46

Figueroa (2006); Consejo Supremo Electoral, 2010.

Table 1.4. South Atlantic Autonomous Region (RAAS): Elected women, ethnicity, and political parties, 1990-2010

ETHNIC GROUP	POLITICAL ORGANIZATION					TOTAL
	FSLN	PIM	PLC [3]	UNO	YATAMA	
Miskitu	0	0	1	0	2	3
Mestizo	10	1	16	2	0	29
Creole	5	0	9	2	1	17
Garifuna	0	0	0	0	1	1
Rama	1	0	1	0	0	2
Sub-total	16	1	27	4	4	52

(Figueroa 2006, Consejo Supremo Electoral, 2010).

From Figueroa's (2006) data, like that of Hodgson (2004), we can also infer that although formal representation inside the regional councils has been achieved, there also exists an over-representation and predominance of certain ethnic groups and a reproduction of gender discrimination. It thus seems as if there are distortions in the electoral proceedings on the Coast that are impeding the effective representation of indigenous and Afro-descended peoples. The over-representation (Miskitus and mestizos in the RAAN and mestizos and Creoles in the RAAS) is perceived by minority indigenous and Afro-descended groups as a negative effect of the autonomy regulations, which they see as having limited their rights, isolated their local communities, and above all decreased their power of decision-making in vital aspects of their survival.

It is also important to note that regional multiethnic political coalitions have either not succeeded or their success has been only relative. In addition, the regional councils frequently have been affected by corrupt and interventionist strategies by the national parties, which tend to control the Supreme Electoral Council in a bi-partisan manner. Cases of corruption in the councils have been documented, but very rarely have there been legal proceedings against officials such that they have been brought to appear in court (Frühling et al. 2007).

Costeño coalitions?
Beyond the categories "indigenous" and "ethnic"

In 2004, I had the opportunity of participating in a study on the political history of YATAMA and its vision of autonomy (Wilson et al. 2008). YATAMA, which stands for *Yapti Tasba Masraka Nanih Asla Takanka* (The Organization of The Peoples of Mother Earth), is an indigenous Miskitu movement/party from the Atlantic Coast of Nicaragua that was founded in 1989.[13] YATAMA originally grouped together a number of the diverse Miskitu indigenous organizations that had struggled in armed conflict against the Sandinista government during the first part of the 1980s (Hale 1994, González 2007).

During the discussion phase of the study, our team (composed of two indigenous intellectuals/activists and myself) had a series of sessions with the six-member YATAMA directorate (five men and one woman). As we were using a collaborative methodology, we wanted to share with them our results and make revisions to our final text. One of the sections of the report that we were interested in discussing with the directorate was the reference the report made to a lack of political will on the part of YATAMA in building multiethnic alliances. It seemed to us that there was a clear resistance on the part of YATAMA to build political coalitions with other ethnic groups on the Coast in the struggle for autonomy, a mandate that is established in the Statute of the organization.[14] The wording in which we had presented the text referring to this issue was as follows:

> YATAMA is perceived as an exclusive organization committed to an agenda of rights that in order to be concretized should be thought of in the multi-cultural context that forms the Caribbean Coast [of Nicaragua]. (Wilson et al. 2004)

This particular formulation of the text provoked a very interesting and somewhat heated debate that permitted us to raise important questions. Several of the YATAMA leaders reacted negatively, saying that the word "exclusive" poorly or simplistically represented a process that was rather more complex. In the first place, they pointed out (with a large consensus, judging by various interventions) that the ethnic hierarchies and tensions between indigenous and non-indigenous people (afro-descendant and mestizos) on the Coast had a historical past and that important differences exist between the groups with respect to their visions, interests, and experiences of struggle around which political cooperation was not something simple to achieve.[15] I transcribe here the intervention by Brooklyn Rivera, principal director of YATAMA, with respect to this point.

> We can open ourselves, as we have done before, in order that non-indigenous candidates can partici-pate on our election slates. But other costeño people should form their *own* organizations with the capac-ity to represent them. If these organizations don't have the strength or the capacity to represent them, then this should be a concern of these communities

13

and not of YATAMA. Including the rights of other
ethnic groups in our struggle would be to drift away
from our principle objective, which is the rights of
indigenous peoples. (Rivera 2004)

"Indigenous peoples and 'ethnics'" (*los étnicos*), as a binominal
conceptual construction, is an expression that emerged during
the meetings and workshops we held with local Miskitu activists
and the political leaders of YATAMA. From my perspective, it
seems that "*los étnicos*" is above all a re-signified category derived
from the Autonomy Statute and it is one that Miskitu activists
and leaders formulated in order to indicate the distinctiveness
of indigenous peoples' collective rights. They articulated these
rights as being founded in their ancestry, in their social history,
and in the continuity of their struggle for autonomy. They see
themselves as The Sons of *Yapti Tasba* (Mother Earth).

In contrast, the Miskitu activists and leaders we spoke to
categorize the "ethnic communities" as the afro-descendants,
i.e., the Garifuna, and Creoles.[16] The status of the mestizos or
ispails (Spaniards) as "ethnic group," however—recognized in
the Autonomy Statute as part of the "ethnic communities"—is
not included in this category.[17] In the discourse of the YATAMA
directorate, "*los étnicos*" can be an open category to designate
(and at the same time differentiate themselves from) other
costeño communities, and it can have the function of demarcating a discourse for legitimizing and specifying the demands for
rights among indigenous peoples, as distinct from those of Afro-
descendants and mestizos.[18] According to Brooklyn Rivera, the
mestizos, as a national ethnic group and the Coast's majority
population, should not be subject to autonomy rights. Moreover,
Rivera indicates that neither do they want to be so subjected:

> In order to be joined together with mestizos we would
> have to form a federation and not an autonomous
> region because when we speak of autonomy, it is
> understood only for indigenous peoples and ethnic
> groups. We believe that mestizos are not interested in
> autonomy because they have never had autonomy—
> only the costeños, the *indigenous* and *ethnic groups*.[19]

I believe that Rivera's interpretation raises various questions that are rarely theorized in the literature about autonomous regions in general and that are also not often discussed in the process of the development of autonomy on the Atlantic Coast of Nicaragua in particular. On the one hand, we can notice the dynamics and factors that impede or facilitate collaboration and interethnic solidarity in the spaces of the multiethnic institutions of territorial self-government that have been established. Additionally, we can observe the elements that propitiate or inhibit processes of supra-regional identity (the conditions of formation of a political community), which has a relationship with the democratic practices of political participation and the degree in which rights are exercised. On the other hand, it is important to underline that the processes of construction of identity based demands for rights, although articulated in a multicultural citizenship regime, can tend to de-legitimize other demands from where new forms of inclusion (for example, of racial type) are formulated.

To me it seems that both questions are closely linked to the visions that the different groups have of what autonomy should be. But also, in the case of Nicaragua, they are related to the institutional design of autonomy, as well as to the institutional design established in order to ensure an inclusive framework of participation of the distinct ethnic groups that form the society of the autonomous regions.

In the case of the Atlantic Coast of Nicaragua, it can be posited as an hypothesis that although the Autonomy Law certainly opened a space of inclusion, this space has been limited by the precariousness with which, in practical terms, the rights of multicultural citizenship are exercised. Although there exists a somewhat generalized perception that the Nicaraguan state should bear the responsibility for the limited way in which autonomy has advanced (IPADE-CASC-UCA, 2004), at the same time we can also see that limited ethnic and gender inclusion has resulted in insufficient political cohesion among costeños. This poses a substantial challenge to their overall participation in the autonomy process. Combined with this reality, some important questions about the cultural and material survival of the communities of the Atlantic Caribbean Coast have been postponed in the contents of the autonomy regulations.[20]

The changes in the ethnic composition of the Coast (today with a large mestizo majority), the negative influence of the national parties in the life of the regional councils, and the exclusion (or limited performance) of multiethnic regional electoral options and alliances are all factors that present obstacles to the development of multiethnic autonomy in its original formulation. I do not intend to create the idea that there has not existed a regional consensus with respect to key themes for consolidating autonomy (for example, political themes about land and education, including higher education), but to show that this consensus has been sporadic and unstable. At the same time, the lack of a consolidated consensus can be seen as an indicator that substantial questions are not channeled through the deliberations of the regional councils. This omission has caused political actors to prefer to channel such questions directly through precarious and pragmatic negotiations with successive national administrations.[21]

Limited inclusion

We have been reflecting on the question of inclusion in the framework of a multicultural citizenship regime. It seems to me that although autonomy has generated new possibilities for inclusion and political participation for indigenous and Afro-descended peoples on the Coast, it is also possible to affirm that costeños have been struggling with a form of limited inclusion. It is limited in two senses.

On one hand, the political institutions that have been created as part of the autonomy regime—in particular the autonomous regional councils—have not fulfilled costeño aspirations for representation and effective participation. But, more specifically, the inclusion of indigenous peoples and ethnic communities in decision-making in vital aspects that concern their survival is still very limited. For example, important decisions of the regional councils that favor the economic activities of multinational firms have negatively affected the rights of the indigenous and Afro-descendant communities.[22] Local political organizations have been gradually or definitively excluded from participation in regional electoral processes (for example, YATAMA, the PPC, etc.). On the other hand, inclusion is limited because the inequalities in participation and political representation between the ethnic groups and also between the genders creates concerns and tensions in a context of an increasing mestizo majority.

These circumstances bring to mind a critique elaborated by Lapidoth (1997) about the negative consequences of the mobility of a population a result of territorial autonomy. Lapidoth tells us that an ethnic majority in a territory can, in fact, be converted into a minority and that such minorities can feel their interests and position to be at an acute disadvantage with respect to the new majorities. Also, Lapidoth calls attention to the risks of conferring rights to a population that does not desire or is not interested in autonomy rights (Lapidoth 1997, 39). The risk is that they will resent a model that has been instituted to guarantee the historic rights of indigenous and Afro-descended people in which they are not included. The result is that a significant part of the mestizo population that today has become established on the Coast and that today is the majority could be concerned with a framework of inclusion that has been imposed on them or that they have involuntarily inherited. Paradoxically, autonomy is an institutional design that has neither successfully reconciled multiethnic coexistence nor guaranteed multicultural rights to indigenous and Afro-descendant people in more than a paper-thin manner.

The implications of this limited inclusion for democracy and the formation of the political collectivity conceptualized in the literature is apparent and resonates with the general reflections of Wolff and Weller (2005) as well as with Gabbert's (2006) observations with regard to the Atlantic Coast case, specifically. That is to say, autonomy regulations by themselves are not sufficient to guarantee genuine governability, political consensus, and/or cohesion among the populations subject to autonomy rights. It seems then that some modifications are necessary for the Nicaraguan costeño autonomy model. What are the tendencies and perspectives that can be observed in the dynamic of the functionality of regional autonomy on the Coast?

A redefinition of the model?
Perspectives with respect to autonomy

In this section, I intend to characterize some of the perspectives with respect to the autonomy process that have implications for its development and consolidation. These perspectives belong to a wider reflection and are linked to previous research I have undertaken (González 2008).

In the first place, a mestizo majority exists, arriving relatively recently from the Pacific region to the Coast, that has very little enthusiasm for the idea of autonomy. For some sectors of this newer mestizo population, autonomy means nothing but the opportunity to express their political preferences in each regional election through voting. However, some of the other older costeño mestizos see that their political rights have been violated in the name of "autonomy" because they have actually been excluded from the right of electing the regional councils. This has been the case even though the areas in which they live—areas where they are an almost absolute mestizo majority—form part of the autonomous regions.[23] This mestizo population lives today mainly in the municipalities of the central region of the Coast, forming a large part of the rural *campesino* (peasant) population. They identify themselves most clearly with a nationalistic narrative and the myth of a Nicaraguan *mestizaje*.[24]

In the second place, we have a multiethnic costeño perspective that is sustained by native inhabitants and residents with historical and cultural roots in the Coast. This population includes indigenous people, Afro-descendants, and costeño mestizos who, although they have differences with respect to what they think autonomy should be and how to strengthen it, coincide in a platform of shared multicultural values. These values include, for example, the importance of costeño unity vis-à-vis the national state, with respect to the right of shared indigenous-Creole territorial areas and the necessity of political representation "without hegemony" in the regional councils.[25] Occasionally, and with relative success, this perspective has intended to construct multiethnic political coalitions in regional electoral processes. This perspective also calls attention to how Afro-descended people consider it important to strengthen their rights, beginning with affirmative action (Cunningham 2006, 74).

A third perspective relates to the indigenous autonomist movement. This movement is politically strong and territorially concentrated. Members of the movement formulate their own demands (for land, indigenous self-government, and political representation) and their own ideas (based in identity and a shared history of struggle). This perspective is more clearly represented by YATAMA, and it does not cooperate easily with the non-indigenous society. It is important to mention that the indigenous autonomist perspective—as well as the multiethnic perspective—represents a population that is today a minority in the territories of the autonomous regions.

Finally, we have to consider the attitudes of the national political elites with respect to costeño autonomy. Juliet Hooker has observed, in my opinion correctly, how a historical continuity exists between the ideologies of Nicaraguan mestizo nationalism and what she calls "mestizo multiculturalism" in times of regional autonomy. This "mestizo multiculturalism," Hooker tells us, resists recognizing the rights of multicultural citizenship for black and indigenous costeños (Hooker 2005, 33).

Following Hooker's line of reasoning, it seems to me that the attitudes of the elites can be distinguished by two currents of thought. For some elites, there exists a *national integrationist perspective*, illustrated most clearly by the leaders of the national liberal and conservative parties, but most strongly by the Liberal Constitutional Party (PLC) whose narrative and nationalist message resonates with the growing mestizo majority on the Coast. From this perspective, autonomy is a failed invention that impedes national unity (Herrera 2001).

For others in the elite sector, we can distinguish an *opportunistic pro-autonomy perspective*, represented most clearly by the FSLN. Re-elected to the national government in 2006, the FSLN has, since 2002, cooperated with the indigenous autonomy movement in its platform of historical demands (González 2007). For the FSLN, this collaboration implies, besides reformulating its initial approach in the multiethnic autonomy that originally inspired the Autonomy Statute in 1987, taking into account the formulations of indigenous autonomy as proposed by YATAMA. I call this perspective "opportunistic" because in my view it is not based necessarily on a strategic commitment to the aspirations of costeños, but on conditioning and subordinating these aspirations to the national political goals of the FSLN.

Conclusions

In the wider Latin American context, autonomy on the Nicaraguan Atlantic Caribbean Coast has been characterized as an innovation without precedent. It has also served as a political and legal model for advancing the recognition of rights of multicultural citizenship to indigenous and Afro-descendant populations historically discriminated against within the framework of national unity and the territorial integrity of the state. My analysis of the interactions and tensions between and among the indigenous peoples and ethnic groups on the Coast in the contest for legitimizing their rights within a limited multicultural regime shows that it is necessary to go beyond the conventional assumption that there is a positive correspondence between democracy and autonomy in the functioning of an autonomy regime. With this caution in mind and in light of revisionist literature about autonomous territories, I have attempted to demonstrate that in the case of the Atlantic Caribbean Coast of Nicaragua the autonomous regional councils are novel instances as spaces of formal political participation for the multiethnic population. However, they are also restricted spaces for influencing, in an effective manner, the fundamental decisions that affect the life and survival of indigenous, afro-descendant, and mestizo costeños.

As part of the political discourse of the leaders of YATAMA, the formulation of an "ethnic" category (*los étnicos*) in order to designate the Afro-descended peoples, at the same time as they judge mestizos as bearing the condition of "non-subjects" of autonomy rights, illustrates this contest for re-signification and challenges the bases of the model of inclusion inaugurated with the Autonomy Statute. The question is more evident today because the Statute in its original conception emphasized a model of multiethnic regional autonomy, thus suppressing the demands of self-government in the indigenous territory. In the context of the contra war, these demands were perceived as potentially divisive (or worse, separatist). It was felt that they could nourish the supremacy of one group over another and, in particular, establish Miskitu hegemony over the rest of the costeño groups. However, changes in the Coast's demographic composition in the last two decades, the lack of interest of the national governments from 1990 in promoting a multicultural rights regime, the still limited advancement in the institutional capacities of the regional councils, and the incongruencies in the mechanisms of political representation have meant that the autonomy regime of the Atlantic Coast has resulted in a limited framework of rights for Afro-descendants and indigenous people and, in addition, has confined the mestizo majority to an imposed model.

Substantively, what appears evident is the exhaustion of an institutional autonomy design that has been neither able to establish multiethnic co-existence nor guarantee the effective realization of multicultural rights for indigenous and Afro-descended peoples. Indeed, these peoples live today in conditions of relative minorities inside the same autonomous regions that constitute their ancestral lands. From here, the panorama in the struggle for the consolidation of rights requires a new outlook, and although it represents new opportunities, the situation is today more complex than when the autonomy regime was first established almost twenty years ago. The situation is complex because of the emerging perspectives that denote both changes in the demographic composition and in its relative representation in autonomous institutions. Thus, we must reassess creatively what has been achieved in the framework of autonomy and what has been advanced in a democratic manner toward its reform. In light of these quandaries, I have posed the idea of a new cycle being initiated in the consolidation of the Nicaraguan multicultural citizenship regime.

Another evident question is that the autonomy regime by itself cannot resolve the problems of asymmetry between groups if they continue to confront barriers that impede fundamental decision-making processes for their development and survival as peoples. For this reason, it will be necessary to develop additional mechanisms of inclusion that reinforce the sense of cohesion and unity of and among the groups, especially around the political collectivity that an autonomous regime tries to institute. This question has relevance beyond the Nicaraguan case and yields important lessons about the theory of multiculturalism and the new forms of inclusion that the diverse countries of Latin America have begun to put into practice.

Notes

1. Translated by Annemarie Gallaugher.

2. The term costeño mestizos is used to refer to long-term Spanish-speaking residents who have developed historical (cultural, familial, etc.) connections to the Coast.

3. This rate includes both natural population growth and incoming mestizo immigration.

4. The literature regarding the factors that precipitated the conflict between the Sandinista revolutionary government and the costeño population is considerable. See the following: Jenkins (1986), Hale (1994), and Frühling et al. (2007).

5. According to Gabbert, the term "*ethnie*" as distinct from "nation," can be understood by taking into account "the special dynamics of ethnicity in societies with little social differentiation and division of labor, owing to lack of infrastructural conditions for state formation." In this sense, "*ethnie*" is a result of the capacity of having access to basic means of subsistence and production for the sustainability of their members. Their reproduction as an independent society relative to the majority society produces distinct political possibilities. On the other hand, the term "ethnic group" is characterized by the "populations that lack the material base for a separate existence because of their embeddedness in an encompassing society. In contrast to *ethnies*, they form an integral part of the processes of production, distribution, and

consumption of that larger society. In contrast to *"ethnie,"* this population [ethnic group] forms an integral part of the processes of production, distribution, and consumption of the wider society" (Gabbert 2006, 94-95).

6. A LASA (Latin American Studies Association) report published in 1986 also takes note of the differences in the types of demands presented on the North and South regions of the Coast. In this report we read: "Zelaya South, because of its different background, has reacted in a distinct manner from the North. In Bluefields, the major concerns were centered on the economic development of the new zone and the importance of acquiring the political characteristics of a new autonomous region. Given the ethnic composition, mostly Creoles and mestizo, with few indigenous elements, the questions of indigenous 'nationhood' were not salient" (Diskin et al. 1986, 31).

7. To these councils we can add the regional representatives for the National Assembly. There are two for the RAAS and three for the RAAN.

8. The Electoral Law combines a system of proportional representation with criteria of ethnic representation. It establishes the election of three representatives by closed political party slates in 15 districts in both autonomous regions for a total of 45 persons elected in each one of the councils. The Law also establishes that in the RAAS, in six of the 15 districts, the slate of candidates for each party must be headed respectively by members of each one of the five ethnic groups that inhabit the region (Miskitus, Sumu-Mayangnas, Ramas, Garifuna, mestizos, and Creoles). By the same logic, in the RAAN, the Law establishes four special districts, from a total of 15, guaranteeing the same ethnic representation of Miskitus, Sumu-Mayangnas, mestizos and Creoles (Asamblea Nacional de Nicaragua 2004).

9. This chart is based on data from the Supreme Electoral Council (1991): Elecciones 1990, República de Nicaragua: Managua; Consejo Supremo Electoral (1995); Elecciones 1994, RAAN-RAAS, Managua: Consejo Supremo Electoral; and URACCAN (2004) with regard to municipal population.

10. The PAMUC was founded in 1997. The party's foundation was preceded by another organization, the MUC (*Movimiento de Unidad Costeña*; Movement for Costeño Unity). The MUC was a Popular Subscription Association which had been founded

by former YATAMA dissidents. The MUC had participated for the first time in the 1996 municipal elections; it won a seat in Waspám's municipal council. The 1995 electoral law instituted the Popular Subscription Association as a flexible political organization able to compete for office in municipal elections. In addition to the municipal level, on the Atlantic Coast they were also entitled to compete for the regional autonomous councils.

11. This chart is also based on data from the Consejo Supremo Electoral (1991, 1995) and URACCAN (2004) with regard to municipal population.

12. According to Hodgson, "In the district of the Ramas, there are 780 persons of this ethnicity registered which corresponds to 19.4% of the total of 4,011 registered in the district. The largest majority ethnicity that voted in that district is mestizo (71.8%) and the second largest majority is Creole (9.42%). A similar case is presented in the district of the Garifuna where there are 765 persons of this ethnicity registered, which corresponds to 31.8% of the total of 2,400. The remaining 68.2% of those registered are mestizo and Creole. This same trend is presented in other districts, such as District Number 8 in the municipality of Pearl Lagoon, where the Creoles elect Miskitus, and in District Number 9 of Corn Island, where the Miskitus have a lot of influence on the results of the election of the Creole ethnicity. In the North Atlantic Autonomous Region similarities are also presented with the Creole of the Municipality of Puerto Cabezas, which must be elected by mestizos and Miskitus, and this situation is repeated with the Sumu-Mayangna in the municipalities of Siuna and Rosita, where an overwhelming majority of mestizos causes each time fewer possibilities for this ethnicity and other minorities to be elected to seats by popular election (Hodgson 2004, 5).

13. I adopt the definition of Van Cott in referring to YATAMA as an indigenous party. According to Van Cott, an ethnic party is: "an organization authorized to compete in elections, the majority of whose leaders and members identify themselves as belonging to a nondominant ethnic group and whose electoral platform includes among its central demands programs of an ethnic or cultural nature" (Van Cott 2005, 3). Van Cott also includes organizations that are self-defined as political movements. YATAMA emphasizes in its platform the communal character of the organization's political struggle. From the point of view of

YATAMA's leaders, this is about doing politics "from a community-based" perspective.

14. The Statute of YATAMA indicates that the organization: "defines the historic right of the indigenous people and ethnic communities regarding their traditional territories and promotes self-government, which will drive the economic, social, and cultural self-development of *Yapti Tasba*, strengthening also a communitarian democracy in the framework of democracy, peace, and the unity of the Nicaraguan nation-state" (Article 2, YATAMA, 1999).

15. In 1997 and 1998, I participated in a working group, which, under the auspices of the Party of the Costeño People (PPC), had attempted an alliance with YATAMA and the Indigenous Multiethnic Party (PIM). The PPC and the PIM are multiethnic organizations with a major base in the southern region of the Coast. The alliance could not be concretized because of a series of factors, among them bureaucratic requirements and the exclusive character of the Electoral Law. In this context, and under a legal plot orchestrated by the PLC and the FSLN, YATAMA was excluded from participating in the municipal elections of 2000. YATAMA sued the Nicaraguan State under the Inter-American Court of Human Rights of the Organization of American States (CIDH) and obtained a favorable sentence in 2005 (Wilson et al. 2008). The PPC had formed an alliance called Costeño Alliance and participated in the regional elections in 1998, winning two elected councilors. In 2005, the PPC lost its legal registry. In the middle of 2008, the PIM was threatened by the Supreme Electoral Council that it would lose its legal registry. At the political level, the PIM has been eclipsed as an independent organization because of its de facto alliance with the PLC.

16. Originally the Autonomy Statute utilized the category "communities of the Atlantic Coast," which included as equal indigenous people, afro-descendants, and mestizos. In the 1995 constitutional reform, the category "indigenous peoples" was introduced in the legislation in order to differentiate them from the afro-descendant and mestizo population, which continued to be identified in the law as "ethnic communities" (Asamblea Nacional de Nicaragua 2000). Law 445 on the communal property regime, approved in January 2003, introduced two important innovations with regard to multicultural recognition. On the one hand, the law states that "ethnic community" should be understood as "the

group of families of Afro-Caribbean ancestry sharing the same identity inherent to their culture, values and traditions related to their cultural roots, natural resources, and forms of land tenure." On the other hand, the law states that an "indigenous community" is "the group of families of Amerindian ancestry settled in a territorial area, sharing a sense identification related to the aboriginal past of their indigenous peoples, and upholding an identity and values inherent to a traditional culture, as well as communal forms of tenure and use of their lands and having their own social organization" (*Gobierno de Nicaragua*, 2003: 78). It is noticeable that the legislation has advanced a differentiated, though subtle, conceptualization of group rights between indigenous peoples and ethnic communities. Under Law 445, mestizos were not included in the category "ethnic community" and instead were relegated to "*terceros*" (third parties), which are: "natural or juridical persons, other than communities, alleging property rights within a communal land or an indigenous territory" (*Gobierno de Nicaragua* 2003, 78).

17. It is interesting to note that in some of these meetings grassroots activists established a distinction between mestizos "from the Pacific" and "costeño" mestizos. The first group was seen by the Miskitu to represent the national state and, thus, the threat of colonization. For that reason, there has been a history of distrust between the two groups. But in the Miskitu perception, the second group, the costeño mestizos, because of their prolonged residence and links to costeño society, were aligned in the struggle for autonomy. This distinction between two types of mestizos is not very clear in the formulations of the members of the political directorate of YATAMA.

18. However, initial documents of YATAMA during the peace negotiations with the FSLN government referred to an alliance of indigenous and Creole people (afro-descendants) as the basis of rights in Yapti Tasba and a central element for reconciliation on the Coast. For example, in 1989 the Peace Initiative proposed YATAMA as a basis for negotiation with the FSLN government, stating that: "Within this process (reconciliation) the historical rights of the Indigenous and Creole peoples to their traditional territories, natural resources, and self-determination should be secured" (YATAMA 1989).

19. Intervention of Brooklyn Rivera during the Territorial Assembly of YATAMA in Pearl Lagoon. Pearl Lagoon, Nicaragua, August

20, 2005. Unedited transcription by Lestel Wilson. Emphasis added.

20. For example, the uncertainties and ambiguities in the autonomy regulations in matters of the usage and control of resources and land tenure have opened the opportunity to commit indigenous rights' abuses. An emblematic case is the community of Awastingni whose communal lands were handed over by the Nicaraguan state in 1996 through a logging concession granted to a multinational firm in order to exploit timber resources. The community, having exhausted the legal proceedings in the national courts, appealed to the Inter-American system of human rights, and in particular to the Inter-American Court of Human Rights (CIDH). The verdict was in favor of Awastingni in the year 2000 and the state was commanded to demarcate and title the lands of the community. In December 2008, the government of Nicaragua granted the title deed to Awastingni. For information about the court legal proceedings, see: http://www.corteidh.or.cr/index.cfm. For information about the demarcation process (including official government documents and title deeds), see: http://www.scaribe.gob.ni.

21. Mirna Cunningham, who played a role as national deputy and delegate of the Nicaraguan President in the North Atlantic Autonomous Region during the first FSLN government, describes this situation in the following manner: "The process of autonomy is still not defined. The Central Government has not supported the process in which the people of the autonomous regions and their authorities have tried to create their own institutionality through political negotiations" (Cunningham 2007, 15).

22. The *Law of Communal Property Regime of the Indigenous Peoples and Ethnic Communities of the Autonomous Regions of the Atlantic Coast of Nicaragua and of the Rivers Bocay, Coco, Indio, and Maiz* (Law, 445) was approved at the end of 2002 and has come to rectify in part this vacuum in the levels of representation and territorial self-government. The Law establishes a procedure for demarcating and titling indigenous and afro-descendant lands, but moreover, it recognizes the forms of authority and territorial government with their own juridical status. This legal development strengthens the level of indigenous and afro-descendant territorial autonomy (*Gobierno de Nicaragua*, 2003).

23. This has been the case of the municipalities of Nueva Guinea, Muelle de los Bueyes, El Rama, and Ayote in which around 50 per cent of the population of the RAAS lives. In national elections, for example, votes from these municipalities are counted to determine the election of regional representatives from the RAAS and the RAAN to the National Assembly. In regional elections, by contrast (and with the exception of Paiwas since 1998), the municipalities do not participate nor are they politically represented in the regional councils. These contradictions have not only led to an increase in demands made by the inhabitants of the area. They have also been exploited by the national political parties. Councilors were also not elected to the regional council in the municipalities of Waslala de Mulukuku in the RAAN, territories in which 25 per cent of the population of the region lives (PNUD 2005, 67-68).

24. "This myth" which, Gould argues, has been a cornerstone of Nicaragua nationalism, has been so believable precisely because it has both "fostered and reflected the disintegration of many Indian communities through migrations and the loss of communal land" (Gould 1998, 9).

25. In 2003, the organization CEDEHCA (Center for Human, Citizen, and Autonomous Rights) carried out several regional consultations to reform the Electoral Law. In the conclusions of their report they indicate that it is necessary: "...to reform the actual Electoral Law so as to realize its meaningful interpretation and recover the spirit and the vision that inspired the Autonomy Statute. [This reform] must be consequential with the recognition of the rights of our indigenous people and African descendants, independent of the size of their population, [or] degree of development, to participate equitably in the construction of an multiethnic and pluricultural democracy." The document proposes the formation of special national indigenous and afro-descendant districts to elect national deputies. In addition, it proposes the creation of such ethnic municipal districts to elect the 45 members of the autonomous regional councils (CEDEHCA 2003, 10, 13). Regarding coalitions for the purpose of demanding indigenous-Creole territorial rights, the work of Goett (2004) on the Rama-Creole territory in the south of Bluefields is important.

26. We can trace, for example, the political history of the PPC, PIM, MAAC, PAMUC and, more recently, Coast Power (The Coast People's Political Movement—*Movimiento Político del Pueblo*

Costeña). This latter organization was founded in 2005 and participated in an alliance with YATAMA in the regional elections in 2006. It won six seats in the council, two of which are Miskitu and four of which are Creole.

27. The PAMUC (Party for the Movement of Costeño Unity, founded in 1997) should also be included in the indigenous movement. Although it articulates an inclusive and multiethnic discourse, it has a mainly Miskitu membership and a presence only in the RAAN. At present, the Supreme Electoral Council has threatened to eliminate the juridical status of the PAMUC, arguing that it did not complete the requirements for registering electoral candidates in the last municipal elections (held in the RAAN in February 2009).

28. The present FSLN government has been surprising for its degree of inclusion of approximately 46 afro-descendant and indigenous costeño representatives (mainly men) in positions, such as important intermediary positions, relevant to the government cabinet. The Vice-Minister of Exterior Relations and at least two national ministers and four vice-ministers are costeños. These form part of what are called the Council for Development of the Caribbean Coast, which is a replacement for (although without substantially changing its mandate) the Secretariat of the Atlantic Coast, created previously by the Bolaños administration. It is still too soon to evaluate if the FSLN move toward inclusion and this new situation by itself will represent a strengthening of the autonomy regime. Also it is possible that this measure has a major relation with the techniques of consociation (Lijphart 1977) in order to accommodate the demands of groups in multiracial societies. I do not mean to say that strengthening the rights of autonomy and the techniques of consociation are intrinsically opposed, but I do leave room for doubt if this is favoring the latter at the expense of a major effort to strengthen the autonomy regime.

Bibliography

Asamblea Nacional de Nicaragua. 1987. *Estatuto de Autonomía de las Regiones de la Costa Atlántica de Nicaragua.* Managua: La Gaceta 238.

Asamblea Nacional de Nicaragua. 2000. *Constitución Política de Nicaragua.* Managua: Editorial Jurídica.

CEDEHCA. 2003. *Propuesta de Reformas a la Ley Electoral de Nicaragua (Ley 331) y Ley de Identidad Ciudadana (Regiones Autónomas de la Costa Caribe de Nicaragua)*. Unpublished document.

CIDCA (Centro de Investigación y Documentación sobre la Costa Atlántica). 1982. *Demografía Costeña: Notas sobre la historia demográfica y población actual de los grupos étnicos de la Costa Atlántica Nicaragüense*. Managua: CIDCA.

Consejo Supremo Electoral. 1991. *Elecciones 1990*. Managua: República de Nicaragua.

Consejo Supremo Electoral. 1995. *Elecciones 1994. RAAN-RAAS*. Managua: Consejo Supremo Electoral.

Consejo Supremo Electoral. 2010. *Declaracion de Electos de Miembros de Consejos Regionales de las Regiones Autonomas del Atlantico Norte y Sur*. Managua.

Cunningham Kain, Mirna. 2006. *Racism and Ethnic Discrimination in Nicaragua*. Center for Indigenous Peoples' Autonomy and Development, CADPI: Bilwi.

Cunningham, Mirna. 2007. La autonomía es un modelo de gobierno para transformar a toda Nicaragua en un país intercultural. Entrevista. *Wani* 50, CIDCA-UCA, Managua, Nicaragua.

Diskin, Martin, Thomas Bossert, Salomón Nahmad and Stefano Varese. 1986. *Peace and Autonomy on the Atlantic Coast of Nicaragua. A Report of the LASA Task Force on Human Rights and Academic Freedom*. Pittsburg: LASA.

Díaz-Polanco, Héctor y Consuelo Sánchez. 2002. *México Diverso. El Debate por la Autonomía*. México: Siglo XXI.

Díaz-Polanco, Héctor. 1997. *Indigenous Peoples in Latin America: The Quest for Self-Determination*. Boulder and London: Westview Press.

Figueroa Romero, Dolores. 2006. *The Quest for Gender Equality: The Participation of Mískitu Indigenous Women in the Autonomous Regional Elections*. Paper delivered at the CPSA Annual Conference. York University, May.

Frühling, Pierre, Miguel González and Hans Peter Buvollen. 2007. *Etnicidad y nación. El desarrollo de la autonomía de la Costa Atlántica de Nicaragua. 1987-2007*. Guatemala: F&G Editores.

Gabbert, Wolfgang. 2006. "Concepts of Ethnicity". *Latin American And Caribbean Ethnic Studies* 1 (1):85-103.

Gobierno de Nicaragua. 2003. *Ley de Régimen de Propiedad Comunal de los Pueblos Indígenas y Comunidades Étnicas de las Regiones Autónomas de la Costa Atlántica de Nicaragua y de los Ríos Bocay, Coco, Indio y Maíz.* Managua-PRODEP (Pograma de Ordenamiento de la Propiedad).

Gobierno de Nicaragua. 2006. *VIII Censo de Población, y IV de Vivienda, Cifras Oficiales, Censo 2005.* Managua, Nicaragua: INEC.

Goett Jennifer. 2004. *PNUD-Informe del Desarrollo Humano de la Costa Atlántica de Nicaragua: Tenencia de las tierras comunales indígenas y afro-descendientes en la RAAS.* Inédito.

González, Miguel. 2007. Los Caminos de *Yapti Tasba*: Autonomía Regional en Nicaragua. In Salvador Marti i Puig, ed. *Pueblos Indígenas y Política en América Latina. El Reconocimiento de sus Derechos y el Impacto de sus Demandas a Inicios del Siglo XXI.* Barcelona: CIDOB.

González, Miguel. 2008. *Governing Multi-ethnic Societies in Latin America: Regional Autonomy, Democracy, and the State in Nicaragua 1987-2007.* PhD Thesis. York University Toronto.

Gould, Jeffrey L. 1998. *To Die in This Way. Nicaraguan Indians and the Myth of Mestizaje, 1880-1965.* Durham & London: Duke University Press.

Hale, Charles. 1994. *Resistance and Contradiction. Mískitu Indians and the Nicaraguan State, 1894-1987.* Stanford: Stanford University Press.

Herrera, Rene. 2001. *Redefinir la Idea de Autonomía.* Managua, Nicaragua: Confidencial 265.

Hodgson D., Johnny. 2004. *Ejes Problemáticos de la Autonomía. Licenciatura en Comunicación Intercultural.* Bluefields: URACCAN. Inedited.

Hooker, Juliet. 2005. Beloved Enemies: Race and Official Mestizo Nationalism in Nicaragua. *Latin American Research Review* 40(3): 14-39.

IPADE-CASC-UCA. 2004. *Percepciones Interregionales en el Pacífico y Atlántico Nicaragüense. Informe de Investigación.* Managua: IPADE-CASC-UCA.

Jenkins Molieri, Jorge. 1986. *El Desafío Indígena en Nicaragua: El Caso de los Miskitos,* México: Editorial Katún.

Lapidoth, Ruth. 1997. *Autonomy. Flexible Solutions to Ethnic Conflicts*. Washington, D.C.: United States Institute for Peace Press.

Lijphart, Arendt. 1977. *Democracy in plural societies: a comparative exploration*. New Haven: Yale University Press.

López Bárcenas, Francisco. 2007. *Autonomías Indígenas en América Latina*. México: Centro de Estudios y Asesoría a los Pueblos Indígenas & MC.

López y Rivas, Gilberto. 1995. *Nacion y Pueblos Indios en el Neoliberalismo*. México: Plaza y Valdes.

PNUD. 2005. *Informe de Desarrollo Humano 2005. Las Regiones Autónomas de la Costa Caribe. ¿Nicaragua asume su Diversidad?* Managua: PNUD.

Rivera, Brooklyn. 2004. Intervención en el taller de devolución de resultados preliminares. Bilwi, Octubre 15. Proyecto Gobernar (en) la Diversidad. Inédito.

URACCAN. 2004. *El Proceso Social y Político de la Construcción de la Autonomía de las Regiones Autónomas de la Costa Caribe Nicaragüense*. Bilwi: PNUD (Informe para el Primer Informe de Desarrollo Humano de las Regiones Autónomas de Nicaragua).

Van Cott, Donna Lee. 2005. *From Movements to Parties in Latin America. The Evolution of Ethnic Politics*. Cambridge: Cambridge University Press.

Wilson, Lestel, Miguel González y Evaristo Mercado. 2004. *Nicaragua: La Experiencia de Lucha de YATAMA en el Proceso de Autonomía de la Costa Caribe de Nicaragua*. Primer Borrador, Quito: Proyecto Gobernar (en) la Diversidad. Octubre.

Wilson, Lestel, Miguel González y Evaristo Mercado. 2008. *Yapti Tasba Masraka Nanih Aslatakanka (YATAMA) en el proceso de autonomía de la Costa Caribe de Nicaragua*. In Xochitl, Araceli Burguete Cal y Mayor and Shannon Speed, coord. *Gobernar en la diversidad: Experiencias Indígenas desde América Latina. Hacia la investigación descolonizada*. México y Quito: FLACSO.

Wolff, Stefan and Marc Weller. 2005. Self-determination and Autonomy: A Conceptual Introduction. Iin *Autonomy, Self-governance and Conflict Resolution. Innovative Approaches to Institutional Design in Divided Societies*, eds Marc Weller and Stefan Wolff. New York: Routledge. 1-25.

Weller, Marc and Stefan Wolff. 2005. Recent Trends in Autonomy and State Construction. In *Autonomy, Self-governance and Conflict Resolution: Innovative Approaches to Institutional Design in Divided Societies*, eds Marc Weller and Stefan Wolff. New York: Routledge, 262-270.

YATAMA. 1989. *YATAMA Peace Initiative*. San José, Costa Rica.

YATAMA. 1999. *Estatutos de Yapti Tasba Masraka Nanih Asla Takanka, YATAMA* Bilwi: YATAMA.

Chapter 2

Incarnation of the National Identity or Ethnic Affirmation? Creoles of Belize[1]

Elisabeth Cunin

———⟨⟨⟨⟩⟩⟩———

" *A h wahn no who seh Kriol no gat no kolcha*" ("I want to know who said Creoles have no culture"). The title of this song by Lee Laa Vernon, famous Belizean artist, reveals the current transformations of the "Creole" status in this small Anglophone country of Central America. Until now, because it was considered the symbol of Belize, the "Creole culture" did not need to be defined, much less defended. This culture was considered to be precisely what bound together a society that was characterized by a multiplicity of groups, described in accordance with their specific origin, history, culture and language. This society was frequently shown as multiethnic, in which the Creoles were the guarantors of integration and "ethnic" labels were reserved for the rest, the "others." Creoles recognized themselves better in their close relationship with power, symbolized by the British Crown and its representatives, colonial administrators and major traders, in a territory that was British Honduras for a long time. Does the fact that

Creoles wonder about their own culture now mean they have to be understood as an ethnic group just like the others? In the way this ethnicity is asserted, are the aspirations of the Creoles to embody the nation, in the way they are considered to have embodied the colony, thereby weakened?

Being the dominant group, the Creoles did not define themselves as an ethnic group; they reserved this label for the "others," those who were not thought to incarnate the Colony, and then the Nation; those who, quoting the expression of Cedric Grant (1976, 19), are *in* the society, but are not *from* this society. In this way, investigations concerning Belize remark upon the tendency to mistake the term "Creole" for "belizeaness". For David Waddell, "the 'Creoles' in general consider themselves the only true British Honduran, and it's the only group that thinks in national terms rather than in racial terms" (Waddell 1961, 71). Assad Shoman confirms this statement: "Creoles are considered the guardians of the British colonial culture, and this culture, with its language, customs and traditions, is considered properly Belizean" (Shoman 1993, 116).

Caribbean societies are frequently described in terms of "creolization," a concept which was defined by Edouard Glissant as "the contact of several cultures or, at least, of several elements from different cultures, in a certain place, that produces a new result, completely unpredictable, in relation with the sum or just the synthesis of these elements" (Glissant 1997, 37). This contact among several cultures not only constitutes an issue of integration of groups defined outside the colonial or national projects but also refers primarily to the power struggles for the definition and the genesis of these projects. In this sense, Belize offers a particularly interesting image: the nation is the object of rivalries among colonial (Great Britain, Spain) and national powers (Mexico, Guatemala) that compete to impose different "societal patterns." This situation seen in a positive light shows the cultural richness of Belize, the coexistence of several languages, the multiplicity of ethnic groups, and so on. When examined less optimistically, this "sitting on the fence" brings isolation – Belize is forgotten by her neighbors of Central America and the often insular Caribbean – and also political anomie which can be linked with the identity and nationalist radicalization associated in this context to any effort to construct a society.

If "creolization" could be considered as the ideological foundation for the independent nations of the Anglophone Caribbean (Bolland 2002, 15-46), it seems, on the contrary, that independence in Belize is a synonym for the stagnation of the political Creole domination and the renewal of identity claims. Many elements –economic, institutional, and diplomatic – explain the difficulties of the Belizean national project; here I will focus primarily upon the terms of ethnization and racialization of the social relationships (De Rudder, Poiret and Vourc'h 2000) to study the contrast amongst apparently contradictory dynamics: integration vs. differentiation, inclusion vs. exclusion, belonging vs. marginalization. I will initially examine the status of "Creole society" associated with Belize to analyze its main characteristics. Then I will concentrate on the social dynamics that hinder the conformation of the "Creole nation" and promote the appearance and development of ethnic-racial differentiation. Finally, I will focus my attention on how, within that context, Creoles have tended to identify themselves as an "ethnic group" to the point of often questioning their own national status.

Belize, a Creole society?

The ambiguity of the category "Creole" was widely described in Belize (Bolland 1990, 29-40) and outside Belize (Jolivet 1990, Dominguez 1986). In Belize, British colonial politics are described generally in terms of "divide and rule:" By dividing the population into ethnic groups with specified outlines and attributes, it was easier to control it and avoid any threatening social mobilization. Within this mosaic, the Creoles have a separate status, due to their proximity to British power. My interest here is to recall that Creoles are considered the "first inhabitants" of the future Belize: the founders of the "*Settlement*" at the mouth of the Belize River at the mid-17th century.

The "Settlement": The Creoles and the others

In chronological terms, the category 'Creole' was not the first used to describe the inhabitants of British Honduras; Karen Judd (1990, 34) considers that it appeared in 1809. It was preceded by the categories "Settlers" and "Baymen" which confirms the local origin of this population and transmits the idea of anteriority and regional connections.In fact, the *Baymen* are considered the first inhabitants of the future Belize, settling in the area surrounding the mouth of the Belize River (in the current place of Belize City). In the mid-seventeenth century, European pirates and traffickers, most of them British, accompanied by Africans and descendents of Africans, slaves or free, took refuge in the coralline islets and the coastal estuaries. Gradually, as the exploitation of the forest wealth became more profitable than attacking foreign vessels, some of them settled down and together constructed a first camp, the *Settlement* (Clegern 1967, Dobson 1973). The development of a viable logging industry as an economic activity led to the continued introduction of slaves (Bolland 1997). Thus, some researchers on Belize believe that Creoles are the result of the meeting between *Baymen* and slaves. The fundamental element is that Creoles define themselves as the "first inhabitants," the founders of the future Belize.

At the same time, the history of Belize is connected to the arrival of the different groups and their settlement in particular places of the territory: Miskitos coming from Nicaraguan coasts in the second half of the eighteenth century; Garinagu, from Saint Vincent Island and from Bay Islands at the beginning of the nineteenth century; *Mestizos* who ran away from the Caste War in the nearby Yucatan state since 1847; Chinese at the mid-nineteenth century and then again at the end of the twentieth century; Indians who came to work on the country northern plantations in the nineteenth century; Mennonites in the 1950s; contemporary African migrants; American pensioners; and as of 1980, political and economic refugees from Central America.

The Battle of Saint George's Caye, starting point of the national narrative

The Battle of Saint George's Caye on 10 September 1798, symbolizes the military victory of the British against the Spaniards and the British occupation of the territory. This is undoubtedly the most revealing event in establishing the status of Creoles and the appearance of a "Creole society," particularly through their different commemorations. Raised to the level of national holiday, 10 September represents the official establishment of the Creole society and the birth certificate of the British Honduras. It is interesting to remark that the independence of Belize occurred on 21 September 1981: That explains why the celebrations on September 10 and 21 are usually mixed up during great part of September and the Battle of Saint George's Caye is implicitly associated to the national independence, as though it were its inspiration. It is necessary to emphasize also that the different groups which would compose the future nation had no role in this mythical episode of the "Belizean identity," either because they had not arrived yet (especially *Mestizos* and Garinagu) or because their presence was denied or ignored (Maya).

The first commemoration of the Battle,[2] on the occasion of the 1898 centenary, symbolizes the affirmation of a "Creole society," in the exact moment when the colony was politically institutionalized and economically developing. Just prior to the celebrations, on 2 April 1898, an editorial of the *Colonial Guardian* brought back the consequences of this victory and drew the edges of the Belizean society: "It guaranteed forever the civil and religious freedom and a good government to the *Baymen* and their descendents and successors. However, beyond the importance of the event itself, the Battle of St. George illustrated a situation in this Colony which is unique in the World History. In all the countries where slavery has existed, the regular condition has always been the slave hatred towards his master, due to the rigor and cruelty of his domination."[3] In fact, the celebrations of 1898 insisted on reminding participants of the "specificity" of Belizean slavery, organized around camps scattered in the forest that allowed certain autonomy to slaves and, in that sense, were shown as completely unconnected with the typical subhuman conditions of slavery in the plantations. This peculiar situation was used as an argument to celebrate the *harmony* of the relationship between masters and slaves, and the emergency of a more pacific society than in any other place. Some years later, Monrad Metzgen (1928),[4] in a compilation book about the Battle of Saint George's Caye, made popular the memory of a fight *shoulder to shoulder*, between the *Baymen* and the slaves.

No man's land and diplomatic rivalries

"The anathema has been indisputable: England stole Belize to Spain, England stole Belize to Mexico, England stole Belize to Guatemala" (Echanove Trujillo 1951, preface). Even in the modern period, statements like this are not unusual in Mexico and especially in Guatemala. Conflicts between the English and Spanish structured the history of Belize within a wider frame of rivalries between the colonial powers in the Caribbean. The territory of Belize was originally attached to the Captaincy of Yucatan that was under the Spanish Crown's control. With the settlement of *Baymen* in the mouth of the Belize River, and specifically with their increasingly numerous and durable incursions into the interior of the land and associated exploitation of the forests, Spain and England signed agreements that granted certain economic prerogatives to the latter, within a territory delimited by the Treaty of Paris (1763). Ultimately disregarded, these agreements demonstrate a pattern subsequently followed by many others that fluctuated according to the degree of tensions between European countries.

However, these diplomatic activities ultimately did not indicate an overriding interest in this territory: Spain did not go farther than the Fort of Bacalar and never placed permanent settlements in Belize; Great Britain waited until 1862 to change the territory into the Colony of British Honduras. With the movement of Latin-American countries toward independence, the negotiations began again, this time with Mexico (to the North) and Guatemala (to the West). The territorial borders were once and for all established with the former (the Mariscal-

Spencer Treaty of 1983) but continued to be a subject of diplomatic conflict with Guatemala (Toussaint 1993).

This conflict, heir of the unresolved tensions amongst colonial powers, is an omnipresent menace to the integrity of Belize and considerably delayed the gradual emergence of independence from the 1960s to 1981. Before the neocolonial ambitions of Guatemala, the (re)affirmation of a Caribbean, Anglophone, and Protestant assumptions which contrast with a Central-American, Spanish speaker, and catholic Guatemala, came the warranty of a yearned independence and the mark of a "Creole society". Either in an implicit or explicit way, the diplomatic conflict with Guatemala led Belize to insist on its Caribbean past more than its Latin-American bonds. Discrediting any integrative discourse, the conflict with Guatemala forced the Creoles to claim a "Belizean specificity" following the logic of defense of a threatened "Creolity." Any identity affirmation, either ethnic or national, must be reconsidered in this strained political-diplomatic context that transforms the marks of belonging in dual and conflictive submissions, pro-Hispanic or pro-British, pro-Central-American or pro-Caribbean.

The failure of the national project of Creolization

With the independence of Belize in 1981, we can wonder if the model of a "Creole society" – in the sense of an integration of the different groups that compose it and a political and cultural hegemony of the Creole group – served as fundamental for the new independent society. The speeches of George Price, the so-called "Father of the Nation," seem to fit perfectly into the search for a society in which differences would be overcome: "There are no Caribs, no Creoles, no Ketchi, Maya or Spanish-Indians. There are only citizens in our country in our own right" (Galvez, Greene 2000, 89). Likewise, he evokes a "handsome blend of people uniting the flesh and blood of Africa, Asia, Europe and of our Carib and Maya origins, but today one people who should remain united to build the new Central American Nation of Belize" (Galvez, Greene 2000, 103). In this way, the anti-colonial movement would not be aligned to ethnic fractures and would have its foundations on a political and socioeconomic line of argument.

But, as we mentioned before, contrary to the rest of the Anglophone Caribbean, independence was delayed for twenty years due to the conflict between Guatemala and Belize. Twenty years passed, during which time the popular movements of the 1960s and 1970s stalled while the English presence became the last barrier towards territorial integrity. To Assad Shoman, one of the main actors of this period, the outcome was bitter: "The system set up by the British and maintained by the two established Belizean political parties had the effect of increasing the country's dependence and perpetuating its state of underdevelopment and denying the people effective participation in the creation of a new society" (Shoman 1987, 49). He argues that, "Independence, therefore, has failed to resolve one of the major goals set by Belize's first political party –the search for, and promotion of, a national identity" (Shoman 1987, 89). When Belize finally achieved its independence in 1981, the situation was very different than the other British colonies in the 1960s: Central America was marked by violent conflicts that had a direct impact on Belize, and Latin America began to look for the development of multicultural politics.

The process of "creolization," which is generally understood as cultural syncretism, served to justify national specificity and unity, could be considered as a threat to the status of the Creoles in their role as heirs of the British power and culture. Therefore, they lost their status of dominant group and their pretension to embody the Nation, politically and culturally.

Black, but not Creoles: Rejection of a part of the black population

Formed on 9 February 1969, the United Black Association for Development (UBAD) movement, initiated by Evan X Hyde, was devised to meet the needs of a double agenda. Permanently mobilizing against the threat of a "latinization" of the country, it adopted racialized speech that denounces the racism of which black populations are victims. The usage of the label "black" refers to the relationships perceived as racial and hegemonic, with a speech inspired widely by the black American movements (from Marcus Garvey to Martin Luther King, including Malcolm X, in an ecumenism that explicitly refused to align to a preset ideology). Curiously, if UBAD had undisputed intellectual and popular influence, it has never been recognized as an institutional actor.[5] In fact, the organization dissolved in 1974, and Evan X Hyde tried unsuccessfully to move into politics with the creation of a party. After the disappearance of the UBAD, his activities shifted toward mass media with the creation of the journal *Amandala* (since 1969) and the radio-television *Kremandala*, then toward education, with the creation of the program *UBAD Foundation for Education*. Evan X then played the role of a severely caustic free electron, cultivating his independence outside any institution. Although the claims of UBAD and *Amandala-Kremandala* were expressed in the anticolonial public scene, and then the national one, these were not integrated into the rising sense of national community. On the contrary, the increasing radicalization of Evan X Hyde's discourse contributed to associate any evocation of the category "Black" to a way of extremism labeled as communist, or even, in an inversion of the allocations, as racist or anti-national.

This is how, far from symbolizing the unity of a "Creole society," Saint George, according to Evan X, favored the division and domination of a Creole bourgeoisie supported by the "British slaveholders". Evan X recalled the history of slaves' rebellions, particularly the one in 1773, and considered these slaves as his true ancestors, much more than the actors in the Battle of Saint George. He therefore re-appropriated the "Black rebel slaves" and re-imagined them as "revolutionary black people". Evan X rejected the category of Creole, yet reproduced the logic of racialization that he at the same time denounced. He called out to the "black" mobilization against any form of "creolization:" "If you are black you think like me. If you're high brown you think like the Loyal and Patriotic Order of the Baymen. If you're white, you couldn't have read so far. You must be thinking black" (Hyde 1995, 17).

Leaning on a populism that would justify his actions (the editorials of *Amandala* are always signed by a "power to the people") and a "conspiracy theory" that would make "Black People" the eternal victims,[6] Evan X Hyde attacks the "*Mestizos*", whom he accuses of wanting to dominate the country, and the Creoles, whom he reproaches for relinquishing to their African heritage and denying their skin color. Therefore, the "Creole" category is called into question by a portion of the population that supposedly belongs to it. To Evan X Hyde:

I am an African-Belizean, I am not a Creole. But I am not an African. I am not going back to farm in Africa, you see. It's like the people who want to divert attention away from the real issues by saying: oh, we're Creole. He acknowledges that they're not white, but they don't want to be African. The history of Belize was that white men exploited black. During all those centuries, the people who came out brown were focused to get a lighter color and there were lots of black women who were disrespected. That's what Creole represents, an attempt to disrespect my Africanness. (interview, April 23, 2008)

New "aliens" and "ethnic war": The Central American migrations

The 1980s met a new wave of migrations with the arrival of Central American refugees fleeing from civil wars in Salvador and Guatemala, and were soon followed by economic migrants from Salvador, Guatemala, and Honduras. Once again, for so sparsely populated a country as Belize, the demographic disruption was massive. The term "alien," used in the nineteenth century by the British colonial administration, reappears in the official language and in the daily interactions, introducing a supplementary degree of strangeness in connection with the category of "migrant." The creation of a refugee camp at Valle de la Paz; the origin of neighborhoods identified as Central-American in origin (Salvapan, Las Flores) in Belmopan, the new capital of the country;[7] the increasing number of people who only speak Spanish; these are some signs that give an especially strong notoriety to this migration. The media has contributed considerably to develop a feeling of insecurity, contrasting the societies of Central America (reduced to a succession of civil wars and military persecutions) with Belize, shown as a peaceful backwater (a "tranquil haven of democracy" as the national hymn celebrates). In this way, the Central-American migrant is frequently described as delinquent, thief, and trafficker.[8] Joseph Palacio goes so far as to talk about an "anti-Central American migrants' ideology in Belize" (Palacio 1990, 6).

Faced with this new migratory wave, the Creole group lost its dominant demographic position; its association (until then taken for granted) with the destiny of the colony and then of the nation was brought into question. Indeed, the 1980s witnessed the merging of two migratory dynamics in direct opposition to one another: While the Central-American refugees arrived in considerable numbers, Belizean people, on the other hand, migrated more and more to the United States. And most of these migrants were Creoles.[9] In fact, in the 1991 census, the *Mestizo* population exceeded the Creole population in number for the very first time: 43.6% of *Mestizos* compared to 29.8% of Creoles.[10] The "ethnic balance" of the country was inverted, as this popular slogan demonstrates: "The Black goes and the Latin comes." This census had many pessimist interpretations that were expressed openly in the form of a "Latin threat" that called into question the "Caribbean identity" of Belize. Harriet Topsey (1987, 1-5) formulated it referring to an "ethnic war." Some years later, the Belizean anthropologist Joseph Palacio (1996) wondered if there was still a place in Belize for what he calls "africanness." Assad Shoman (1993, 121) mentioned a project destined to favor the Haitian migration: "people of much more unconnected customs and language to the Belizean than those of the Central-Americans, but dark skinned."

It is essential to note that the categories of the census account more for the social rules in the administrative or political camp than a "reality" they should "reflect." The extensive nature of the category *Mestizo* favors the feeling of a Hispanic "invasion, since it forgets the multiplicity and heterogeneity of the population included in this category. It indeed reunites the victims of the Caste War of the nineteenth century and the Central American refugees of the 1980s under the same appeal. Without a shadow of a doubt the criteria of the administrative classification had, willingly or not, a fundamental consequence in the institutionalization of this new *Mestizo* face of the country. Numerous "scaremonger" interpretations of the 1990s were based on a methodical comparison of the census of 1991 and 1981, assuming continuity among categories. However, in 1981, respondents were asked to choose from different options, namely the terms "Negro/Black" and "mixed," categories most often reinterpreted afterwards as synonyms of Creole and *Mestizo*.

Multicultural politics and ethnization
The Maya and the Garinagu

The period that preceded independence was characterized by a backward motion of ethnic matters in favor of the promotion of a common "national identity" and the rejection of the British policy of "divide and rule." The work *A History of Belize. Nation in the Making*, the first independent national narrative, describes the actions of the colonial administration as follows: "people were also divided by their religion, by where they lived, by occupation, by color and by class (...). Each group was encouraged to hate and fear the others" (*A History of Belize* 2004, 69). However, the 1980s and 1990s witnessed a renewed affirmation of the ethnicization of certain groups, mainly Garifuna and Maya. Scholars should consider the appropriation of ethnic identities that operated until then as a hierarchal assignation instead. Beyond the geographical and social limits, the ethnicization re-asserted differences, even if the second logic is far from having completely replaced the first one. The appearance of two organizations of an ethnic nature, the *National Garifuna Council* (in 1981) and the *Toledo Maya Cultural Council* (created in 1978, but above all active in the mid-1980s), was symptomatic of these transformations. If their ethnicization was a synonym of marginalization and inferiority before, now it became an identity vector enhanced by the Maya and Garifuna populations themselves in the new multicultural globalized context of the 1980 and 1990s.

That is how many works propose an analysis in terms of preservation of specific ethnic traits: "In the face of persistent and ever-increasing forces of change, these groups have managed to retain their cultural cohesiveness to a substantial degree, and all possess a strong sense of shared identity" (Wilk, Chapin 1990, 5). In the case of the Garinagu, the existence of a specific language, the religious rites (*dugu*), the transnational community (Honduras, Guatemala, Nicaragua, Belize, and United States), the richness of the musical practices (*paranda, punta, punta rock*), are used as a line of argument to highlight their difference and their "authenticity" (González 1969, Foster 1986, Cayetano and Cayetano 1997, Izard 2004, Palacio 2005). Their peculiar history places them in an ambiguous identity situation since they can be classified (and they classify themselves) as indigenous and as African descendants. All the more reason for us to say that they are identified in ethnic terms, in that ethnicity is a factor that they in fact cultivate and that is widely recognized. The Garinagu language, dances, and chants received the status of Intangible Cultural Heritage of Humanity by the UNESCO in 2001.

While the *Toledo Maya Cultural Council* works above all on the valorization of the Maya history and culture, it took advantage of the development of patrimonial tourism (exploiting the Maya archaeological and natural sites) and engaged in a newfound course; as it is shown in the debates about the creation of a "Maya homeland" in the 1980s or its participation in a network of Mesoamerican Maya NGOs.

Despite this re-ethnicization, which was sometimes described in terms of the blooming of a "multicultural folklore" (Macpherson 2007, 17) these changes have an unquestionable political dimension. This is not expressed through an explicit political commitment (political parties, ethnic vote, specific claims), but rather has served to contribute to further weaken the model of "Creole society" that had been established on the basis of a marginal inclusion from the Garinagu and the Maya: as Belizean citizens who did not incarnate the Belizean Nation. Furthering this shift, the *Toledo Maya Cultural Council* states that the Maya were the first inhabitants of Belize before they were pushed to the margin. The memory of the existence of a particular way of political organization (the *Alcaldes* institution inherited from the Spanish colonization, Bolland, 1988), having survived what is presented as an invasion of the British colonists, primarily the *Baymen*, or the petition for creating a "Maya homeland," an indigenous reserve in the South of the country, demonstrates the extent these changes have gone in opposing a strictly cultural identity confinement. We will underline equally the fact that the Garinagu had founded a *Settlement Day* that celebrates their arrival to Belizean lands in 19 November 1802; in this way they too become established in the national territory like the first *Settlers*, the Creoles, did. The anniversary of the Garinagu's arrival was promoted to "national holiday" level in 1977; the same level as Independence Day, the Battle of Saint George and "Día de la raza", renamed "Panamerican Day", which, in Latin America, celebrates the arrival of the Spanish to American lands (12 October) and which is associated to the *Mestizo* population in Belize.

In a general way, this ethnicization, from now on positive, has effected change in national politics and staging. For example, in 2007 the National Library opened its doors to a presentation of the Garifuna culture and history while the National Museum presented an exhibition about the Maya, which showed chiefly a jade mask discovered in 1968 by the American archeologist David Pendergast in the site of Altun Ha. It was accompanied by the following comment: "It is a unique relic bequeathed to us by some of the first Belizeans." It is interesting to recall that this museum, opened in 2000, only traced the history of the country from 1705, the date of the settlement of the British colonists to exploit wood, to the present day in its chronology. While the Maya civilization was celebrated in the second floor, it remained forgotten in the first floor.

Likewise, in 2004, a national project concerning the overhaul of the educational programs and the integration of a "multicultural" element in their curricula was launched. Supported by the Ministry of National Education and the *National Institute for Culture and History*, this initiative will lead to a publication with the programmatic title: *Belize New Vision. African and Maya Civilization. The Heritage of a new nation.* The reconsideration of a national identity, which exceeded initial differences, just as the "fathers" of the independence upheld it, is evident:

"The multi-cultural model looks at Belize's cultural heritage in a multifaceted and holistic perspective. It seeks to develop an awareness of the different cultures that are manifest in present day Belize (...). The multi-cultural model is an attempt to link Belize's history to the different home lands from whence the different cultures came" (Iyo, Tzalam, Humphreys 2007, 85). This new "multicultural vision" from now on only considers the categories "African" and "Maya". In this way, the colonial and national epochs seem to be put in parentheses for the benefit of a return to a distant precolonial origin, in which "Creoles," "Garinagu," and "Blacks" would be mixed into one group, the "Africans," reducing the current heterogeneity of the populations of African descendants (even though the African populations, in Africa, are presented in great detail). The "history of Belize," the one that began as a construct in the 17th century and prevails today in the national narrative has been reduced to occupy the third section of the work, after the Maya history and culture and then the African contribution to a lesser degree. Above all, any trace of a society dominated by a Creole group favoring the integration seems to have disappeared, in a relationship of horizontality among the different sectors of the population.

Towards the ethnicization of Creoles?

Today's multiethnic language defies the definition of the Creole group: Is it an ethnic group like the others? Has it lost its special, preponderant place, personifying the nation? The "Latin threat" and the "re-ethnicization" of the Garinagu and the Maya, far from leading to the vanishing of the Creole group, tend to promote its "salience" (Douglass, Lyman 1976) in a logic of withdrawal over ethnic traits. The "Creole" category appears in the 1991 census in a revealing way: the Creole people are no longer the symbol of the Colony or the Nation. Instead, they have become an ethnic group like the rest. In other words, the national project is less similar to a creolization process – understood as the integration of differences – than to a progressive politicization of ethnic membership inherited from colonial times and translated to the specific context of the end of the twentieth century. In this logic of differentiation, the Creoles have to justify a particular culture, language, and history, while their "natural" association with the collective project is called into question.

Redefining their place

To illustrate this process, an examination of the 2005 re-publication of a manuscript by Lawrence Vernon is revealing. The manuscript was originally written in 1964 to get his college diploma.[11] The foreword highlights the importance of this work, republished during the 70th anniversary of the *Belize National Library* and in response to a particularly strong petition (Vernon 2005, forward). Lawrence Vernon, who comes from a great Creole family, was connected with the National Library. Now, forty-one years later, the text has changed. First of all, the whole title adopted a more "politically correct" language, changing from *A Brief ethnological description of Belizean races* to *Cultural Groups of Belize*. Additionally, the order for presenting these groups and the number of pages devoted to each one, vary from one edition to the other: while in 1964 those qualified as "*Spanish community*", "*Spaniards*" or "*Meztizos*" occupied the fourth position, right after the Maya, Garinagu, and Creoles, and had only three pages devoted to them, they now open the 2005 publication. Also, in the 1964 edition, right after describing the Garinagu and Maya, Vernon states that the other groups to be studied – including the Creoles – do not show clear enough differentiation markers, and the author seems to be in some doubt regarding their status: "The following races of people that help to comprise the population of the country are not a 'tribe' as such (...), but rather regarded as more conventional or conservative people who have to a great extent adopted Western ways and culture" (Vernon 1964, 70). The description of the Creole category is also instructive. If both texts coincide in the main traits (African ascendancy, harmony between masters and slaves, a connection with Belize City), several nuances are revealing. The long series of stereotypes that depicted the Creoles in 1964 disappeared: "The average Creole has an apparent smile, and laughter is usually not far under the surface. He tends to be outspoken and vociferous in his talking, and always ready for a fight. His willingness to help is another of his fine qualities, and his friendliness to all is quite evident (...)" (Vernon 1964, 71). The "black blood" (Vernon 1964, 72) is replaced by "African blood" (Vernon 2005, 22). The affirmation of the Belizean identity of the Creoles, "generally accepted as the finest example of a true Belizean" (Vernon 1964, 71) produces a more tinged discourse: "because of their colorful intermixture, and having occupied the largest center of population in Belize, the Creole has perhaps adapted the most nationalistic attitude among cultural groups" (Vernon 2005, 23) While the permanency of a racial hierarchy is underlined in 1964, "the upper class of Belize society remains light-skinned, and the number of upper class negroes are small" (Vernon 1964, 74) the 2005 text adopts a more cultural perspective: "of all present-day Belizeans, it is the Creole who is likely the most culturally alienated and confused for it was the African, the Creole's ancestor, who was most intensely dehumanized, de-culturized, and reoriented" (Vernon 2005, 23). This cultural alienation leads to the extinction of the "popular beliefs" (Vernon 2005, 28) and almost the entire disappearance of religious practices (Vernon 2005, 29), but it authorized the prevalence of specific music and dances: "despite efforts by the slaves-masters to suppress music that they considered a nuisance, or an encouragement to revolt, the *Gombay* as a musical recreational event survived and was recreated in today's Boom-and-Chime bands" (Vernon 2005, 28). In 1964, however, the same author stated that the "the Mayas have their Deer dance, the Caribs their *Cunjoy* and *Sambai*,[12] while the Creoles have no set dance" (Vernon 1964, 77).

The language shifted from focusing on racial matters to a much more cultural focus. Similarly, some cultural practices that would be common to the Creoles reappear and replace a characterization based primarily on social traits. Additionally, the national status of the Creole group, held like evidence before, becomes the order of a "behavior" which is not perfectly assured by itself.

Ethnic... but not too much

Several years after the creation of the Garinagu and Maya *Councils*, the Creoles adopted, in 1995, their own association, the *Kriol National Council*, and they seem to want to be included in this logic of ethnicization. "The purpose of the National Kriol Council of Belize is to promote the culture and language of the Kriol people of Belize, as well as harmony among all the ethnic groups of Belize.. The first words in the *National Kriol Council* website (http://www.kriol.org.bz/) are revealing: on one side, the spelling used leaves the term "Creole" out of the English orthographic rules; on the other, the "Kriol" define themselves in ethnic terms like culture and language. At the same time, however, they are still presented as the ones guaranteeing harmony between the different ethnic groups. This role as arbiter or conciliator is not new, but it is no longer connected to the proximity of the British power, and it seems to adhere strictly to an ethnic logic. In fact, the website is divided in three sections which present "Kriol" culture, history and language.

The page concerning culture starts with a question: "What is a 'Creole'?" and it seems to participate in a classification process that appears geared toward the division of ethnic groups. The answer, however, far from giving a series of identification criteria, offers an extremely open and subjective definition of the Creole category. In the same manner, there is a return to the usual spelling of this ethnic group, accentuating the normalization in detriment of the differentiation:

> There are many answers to this question and we do not intend to present a complete definition. The following categories discuss cultural qualities that are identified as Creole. However, in the final evaluation, while an outsider might look at someone who embodies many of these characteristics and say that person is a Creole (and there are people who will say that a certain person doesn't embody one of these qualities enough, i.e. he isn't black enough to be a Creole), anybody who holds to some of these qualities and wants to identify as a Creole – can be Creole. (http://www.kriol.org.bz/CulturePages/Creole_Culture.htm).

Although the ethnic specificity is presented as an argument, the definition criteria for this ethnicity are extremely vague; even if we could expect a sort of identity withdrawal, the ethnicity conception transmitted is absolutely inclusive.

Indeed, the words of Mirna Manzanares (interview from April 19, 2008) and of Silvana Woods (interviews from November 8, 2007 and April 17, 2008), President and Secretary, respectively, of the *National Kriol Council,* confirm the coexistence of these inclusion and exclusion logics. It was observed at that time that an important effort was taking place to valorize a culture presented specifically as Creole which would take inspiration directly from Africa: lexicon and cuisine considered as African; promotion of the *Sambay,* described as an African fertility chant; support to the story-tellers and oral tradition associated with Africa, etc. Every year, during May, the *Cashew Festival* is organized in the town of Crooked Tree. The festival is intended to celebrate the Creole culture. It is not about the city of Belize anymore, former symbol of both "Belizeaness" and "Creolity," perceived today as too mixed. The Creole culture is situated in the old timber camps that border the rivers (Belize River, New River) that were the main communication and timber transportation routes in the past. These small villages are presented as the true birthplaces for a specific culture, in which we would find the Creole language, *bruckdown* music, cashew wine or Christmas festivities. In that way, this "back to the origins" passes through a search for authenticity expressed by a valorization of rural life, a reaffirmed reference to Africa, and an exaltation of the woodcutter figure, which replaces that of the slave. At the same time, M. Manzanares and S. Woods stress the "inter-ethnic harmony," the importance of the mixed races from which, the Creoles would be a symbol. The interviewees repeat in several occasions that anyone can become a member of the *Kriol Council* if they share the Creole culture, it does not matter if they are Chinese, *Mestizo* or Mennonite. Even though the Creole culture is not as visible as others, that is exactly why it is "so much a part of everything," a "living culture" that "everyone experiences in daily life," for which it seems "evident," "incorporated," and "present everywhere."[13]

Conclusion

In April 22, 2008, Lee Laa, "the Queen of *Kriol kolcha*" was invited to participate in the Earth Day celebrations in Guanacaste National Park, at the entrance of Belmopan. She was wearing an African dress with the colors of the Union Jack, and she sang some themes accompanied exclusively by her own compact discs played in a portable sound system. When she was about to sing the classic "Kriol Kolcha," she asked the improvised DJ to lower the volume and then she gave a long explanation on the origins of the slaves, the mixes with British people, the timber camps, the Creole language, etc. Off the improvised stage, Lee Laa recalled the speech, saying that "people tell me that I'm wasting my time, that Creoles don't have history or culture. They are wrong" (interview, April 22, 2008). We are therefore led to believe that this is about presenting and valuing the Creole culture and history. But, in doing so, is not the Creole place among society what ends up transformed? The more the Creoles adhere to an ethnic group, the less they can represent the nation; on the contrary, the less they are defined in ethnical terms, the more they will be able to maintain their preponderant position. That is how they are confronted with this contradiction: to lead the national project reaffirming a specific identity and to defend a culture that is threatened even though it is supposed to symbolize the national culture. Therefore it becomes apparent to what extent the Creole representatives' discourse seems to be trapped in a contradiction, between affirmation of a cultural specificity and the logic of crossbreeding, between the valorization of a difference and normalization, between singularity and daily life.

Bibliography

A History of Belize: Nation in the Making (Benque Viejo del Carmen: Cubola Productions, 2004 [9th edition]), 69

Bolland, Nigel. 1986. *Belize. A New Nation in Central America.* Boulder and London: Westview Press.

Bolland, Nigel. 1988. *Colonialism and resistance in Belize: essays in historical sociology.* Belize City: SPEAR.

Bolland, Nigel. 1997. *Struggles for freedom: essays on slavery, colonialism and culture in the Caribbean and Central America.* Belize City: Angelus Press.

Bolland, Nigel. 2002. Creolisation and Creole Societies. A Cultural Nationalist View of Caribbean Social History. In Shepherd & Richards, eds. *Questioning Creole. Creolisation Discourses in Caribbean Culture.* Kingston: Ian Randle Publishers, Oxford: James Currey Publishers: 15-46.

Cayetano, Sebastian, Cayetano, Fabian. 1997 [1990]. *Garifuna history, language and culture of Belize, Central America and the Caribbean. Bicentennial Edition (April 12th 1797 – April 12th 1997).* Belize: BRC.

Clegern, Wayne. 1967. *British Honduras: Colonial dead end, 1859-1900.* Baton Rouge: Louisiana State University Press.

De Rudder, Véronique, Poiret, Christian, Vourc'h, François. 2000. *L'inégalité raciste. L'universalité républicaine à l'épreuve.* Paris : Presses Universitaires de France, collection Pratiques théoriques.

Dobson, Narda. 1973. *A History of Belize.* London: Longman Caribbean, Trinidad and Jamaica: Longman Caribbean Limited.

Dominguez, Virginia R. 1986. *White by Definition: Social Classification in Creole Louisiana.* New Brunswick: Rutgers University Press.

Douglass, William ans Stanford, Lyman. 1976. L'ethnie : structure, processus, saillance. *Cahier International de Sociologie* LXI: 197-220

Echanove Trujillo, Carlos A. 1951. *Una Tierra en Disputa (Belice ante la Historia).* Mérida: Editorial Yucatanense Club del Libro.

Foster, Byron. 1986. *Heart drum: spirit possession in the Garifuna communities of Belize.* Belize: Cubola.

Galvez, Francisco Jr., Greene, Edward. 2000. *George Price. Father of the nation of Belize.* Belize: Ion Media.

Glissant, Edouard. 1997. *Traité du Tout-Monde. Poétique IV.* Paris : Gallimard.

González, Nancy. 1969. *Black Carib household structure.* Washington: University of Washington Press.

Grant, Cedric H. 1976. *The Making of Modern Belize: Politics, Society and British Colonialism in Central America*. Cambridge: Cambridge University Press.

Hyde, Evan. 1995 [1969]. Knocking Our Own Thing. In Evan Hyde, *X Communications*. Belize City: The Angelus Press Ltd

Iyo, Aondofe, Tzalam, Froyla, Humphreys, Francis. 2007. *Belize New Vision: African and Maya Civilizations. The heritage of a new nation*. Belize City: Factory Books,.

Izard, Gabriel. 2004. Herencia y etnicidad entre los Garífuna de Belice. *Revista Mexicana del Caribe* 17: 95-127.

Jolivet, Marie-José. 1990. La créolisation en Guyane. Un paradigme pour une anthropologie de la modernité créole. *Cahiers d'Etudes Africaines* 37(48): 813-837.

Judd, Karen. 1990. Who will define US? Creolization in Belize. *SPEAReport* 4: 29-40.

Macpherson, Anne. 2003. Imagining the Colonial Nation: Race, gender, and Middle-Class Politics in Belize. 1888-1898. In Nancy P. Appelbaum, Anne S. Macpherson, Karin Alejandra Rosemblatt, eds. *Race and Nation in Modern Latin America*. Chapell Hill and London: The University of North Caroline Press: 108-131.

Macpherson, Anne. 2007. *From Colony to nation. Women activists and the gendering of politics in Belize, 1912-1982*. Lincoln and London: University of Nebraska Press.

Monrad Metzgen, ed., *Shoulder to shoulder, or the Battle of St. George's Caye 1798* (Belize City: Literary and Debating Club, 1928).

Palacio, Joseph. 1990. Socioeconomic integration of Central American immigrants in Belize. *SPEAReports* 2.

Palacio, Joseph. 1996. Is there any future for Africanness in Belize?. *Journal of Belizean Affairs* 1(1): 34-47.

Palacio, Joseph. 2005. *The Garifuna. A nation across the border. Essays in social anthropology*. Belize CA: Cubola Books.

Sheperd, Verene. 2002. "Questioning Creole: Domestic Producers and Jamaica's Plantation Economy". In Shepherd & Richards, eds. *Questioning Creole. Creolisation Discourses in Caribbean Culture*. Kingston: Ian Randle Publishers, Oxford: James Currey Publishers: 167-180.

Shoman, Assad. 1987. *Party politics in Belize. 1950-1986.* Benque Viejo del Carmen: Cubola Productions,.

Shoman, Assad. 1993. La inmigración centroamericana en Belice: un choque cultural. In Francesca Gargallo, Adalberto Santana, comp. *Belice: sus fronteras y destino.* México: Universidad Autónoma de México.

Shoman, Assad. 2000 [1994]. *Thirteen chapters of a history of Belize.* Belize City: The Angelus Press Limited.

Toussaint, Mónica. 1993. *Belice: una historia olvidada.* México DF: Instituto Mora – Centro de Estudios Mexicanos y Centro Americanos.

Topsey, Harriot . 1987. The ethnic war in Belize. *First annual studies on Belize conference.* Belize City: SPEAR Ethnicity and Development: 1-5.

Vernon, Lawrence. 1964. *A Brief ethnological description of Belizean races.* Belmopan: National Archives, Unpublished Master.

Vernon, Lawrence. 2005. *Cultural Groups of Belize.* Belize: Print Belize.

Waddell, David. 1961. *British Honduras: A historical and contemporary survey.* London, New York and Toronto: Oxford University Press.

Wilk, Richard, Chapin, Mac. 1990. Ethnic minorities in Belize: Mopan, Kekchi and Garifuna. *Speareports* 1.

Notes

1. Translated by Karla Sánchez Domínguez and Ernesto Du Solier Espinosa. Revision by Katrina Keefer.

2. The first representations of the Battle of Saint George appear in 1823: After a slaves' rebellion, the Creole elite finds out about the benefits of promoting a reference to a "harmonious society" before the slaves and the British managers.

3. *Colonial Guardian*, April 2, 1898.

4. For a critical analysis see (Shoman, 2000; Macpherson, 2003).

5. In this regard, Belize's situation is quite different from that of Jamaica. See (Sheperd 2002).

6. Beyond this discourse, it's necessary to state that Evan Hyde comes from a prominent Creole family and he himself held one of these institutional positions which he is so inclined to criticize, since he was senator from 1993 through 1998.

7. In addition, since its creation at the beginning of the 1960s, it struggles to develop and populate itself, which accentuates even more the feeling of Central American "invasion".

8. In that regard, the 2000s are witness of an inversion of the tendency: the media generally will associate violence, particularly severe in Belize City, to the black shown as young people out of work, consumers and traffickers of drug.

9. The first important migratory flows to the United States date from the beginning of the 1960s, after the hurricane Hattie (March, 1961), which devastated a great part of Belize City, most of it Creole.

10. The census of 2000 (the last one available) confirms this tendency: while "Creoles" are approximately the 24.9% of the population, those who are grouped from now on in the category "Mestizo/ Spanish" represent the 48.7% of the population.

11. The photocopied document is available at the Belmopan archives, in the *Books* category, referenced as 0069 BAD.

12. It is likely that the 2005 "gombay" is the 1964 "sambai", now associated with the Creoles and spelled "Sambay" or "Sambai".

13. It's interesting to mention that I heard a very similar speech during my visit to the *Creole Museum*, in Belize's downtown, and whose managers also participated in the rise of a Creole mobilization in the 90s. The Museum portrays a "typical" Creole home of a family living from cutting limber. There, and above all, the "Creolity" seems to express itself in daily life much more than in any political claim or in cultural traits set on stage.

Chapter 3

Genesis of Transnational Networks: Afro-Latinamerican Movements in Central America[1]

Carlos Agudelo

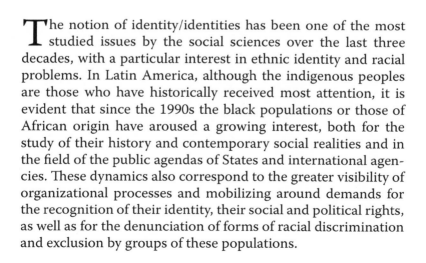

The notion of identity/identities has been one of the most studied issues by the social sciences over the last three decades, with a particular interest in ethnic identity and racial problems. In Latin America, although the indigenous peoples are those who have historically received most attention, it is evident that since the 1990s the black populations or those of African origin have aroused a growing interest, both for the study of their history and contemporary social realities and in the field of the public agendas of States and international agencies. These dynamics also correspond to the greater visibility of organizational processes and mobilizing around demands for the recognition of their identity, their social and political rights, as well as for the denunciation of forms of racial discrimination and exclusion by groups of these populations.

It is in countries like Brazil and Colombia where this phenomenon can be observed with more vigor although in the rest of the region similar processes occur with a greater or lesser degree of intensity.[2] Central America is not the exception, as over a superficially quite small area, divided into a number of different countries, there is a black population diversified in its history and social and political dynamics: Garifuna, Creoles, immigrants from the Antilles, etc. Each country has developed its own inclusion and exclusion mechanisms. Demographically, the Central American Afro-descendent population is of minor importance. However, in practically all the countries in the region, from Belize to Panama (with the exception of El Salvador), there is a quite significant process of political mobilization through which black leaders and movements have achieved the inclusion of their demands in national and global political agendas.

Most of these movements articulate themselves around ONECA/CABO – Central American Black Organization. CABO defines itself as a network of Central American Afro-descendent organizations, "... that work to promote the overall development of the Afro-Central American peoples and communities from the human rights perspective, in all our actions aiming towards unity in diversity, equality of gender, ethnic group and race amongst human beings and frontal combat against racism and discrimination."[3]

It can be said that there is currently a "discursive symbolic and transnational space for demands" amongst Latin American black peoples in which local and national processes obtain feed-back from those generated on a scale that transcends the borders of each country and the sub-region. CABO belongs to this dynamic. This space constitutes a field for the "accumulation of forces" that for some moments in time becomes the most important scenario for the development of the movements acting within it. One of the forms of action and relation assumed by some of the Latin American black movements in this transnational space goes through what are commonly called "networks." This widely used concept has been assumed spontaneously and "naturally" as the most efficient mechanism of action, if not the only one possible, in today's globalized world.

The concept of "networks" has been used in the social sciences since the 1950s and from then on has spread irregularly within and onto the frontiers of these disciplines (Mercklé 2004). Since the 1980s and 1990s its use has become generalized to define forms of interaction between different types of social actors with characteristics and fluidity than those of more structured, conventional forms of association. One of the deciding factors in the multiplication of this term applied to certain social relationships is the symbol of the "great network that unites the world (Internet)." Technological power and the multiplication of forms of circulation, control of information and its incidence on mechanisms for the regulation of economic, social and political processes lead some analysts to see in *networks* a new planetary social paradigm.[4]

Our research on what we call "transnational networks of black movements in Latin America" is work in process. In this overall framework, we have begun a study on Central America in which CABO, as a network, is one of our main points of interest.

The main purpose of this text is to explore the aspects that constitute the background of such networks and present some of their characteristics. To do this we will begin with the period when these political dynamics emerged on the transnational scene. We will highlight the strategic role of international agencies that incorporate the black populations into their policies as part of their discourses in which globalization is articulated with the recognition of multiculturalism, protection of biodiversity, and "democratic governability." After that, we will present elements on the way the main networks of black movements in Latin America are being constructed, their particular features. and the actors participating in the process of construction and action. We end this paper with a series of reflections on their functioning, potential, and limitations.

The data we are using as a basis for this reflection are still in the process of collection and analysis. As well as information on CABO, some of the elements that serve as a starting point for this study come from an analysis of the black social and political movement in Colombia.[5] Those concerning other Latin American countries and other spaces important for transnational dynamics come from other sources to which we will refer.

Some background elements

In the 1990s, as a result of the confluence of national and international factors, important changes in the situation of political "invisibility" of the black movements became evident. Organizational processes that sped up the demands of these movements became part of national political agendas. In various countries, constitutional reforms were made that included specific rights for the black populations (Nicaragua, Brazil, Colombia and Ecuador). In others, laws were passed or official agencies were created with regard to their populations of African origin (Honduras, Guatemala, Panama, Peru and Uruguay).

These reforms occurred in the framework of the recognition of multiculturalism and diversity in national societies. Up until this moment, these countries had been conducted under a universalist discourse and the vindication of their character as *mestizo* republics (Wade 1993, 1997, 1999, Gros 1997). The reduced space for the recognition of otherness was occupied almost exclusively by the indigenous peoples.

In the context of the recognition of ethnic diversity in Latin America, the central protagonists will continue to be the indigenous peoples. Since the 1970s, the indigenous movement has gradually been consolidated. Some black movements are inspired by the example of indigenous mobilization to defend their rights.[6] The energy behind this dynamic process towards visibility is to be found in the new dimension emerging in Latin America in the light of the struggles of the black movements in the United States, the defeat of *apartheid*, the mixture of images of political leaders, artists and sportsmen like Malcolm X, Martin Luther King, Nelson Mandela, Bob Marley and Michael Jordan. Cultural expressions like *reggae, rap,* and *hip hop* join the revival of Africa as an imaginary identity of origin for the black peoples of the world (Sansone 1998, 2000). In this context, the local processes of historical resistance to slavery acquire a new dimension – runaway slaves, their spaces of resistance (palenques, rochelas, cumbes and quilombos or the case of the

Garifuna people who resisted slavery from the start by escaping from the slave ships[7]), and their leaders. The most visible case is that of the Zumbi and the Quilombo of Palmares in Brazil. In Central America there is Satuyé, the leader of Garifuna resistance on the island of San Vicente, but other similar figures also became current symbols of the mobilization.[8]

Projects like "The Slave Route" promoted by UNESCO from 1994 onwards and the "World Conference against Racism, Racial Discrimination, Xenophobia and Related Intolerance," organized by the UN in Durban, South Africa in 2001 and the preparatory meeting for Latin America and the Caribbean, held in Santiago, Chile in 2000, constitute transnational spaces from which the process of the unprecedented increase in the production of discourses, demands, mobilization, intellectual and political leaderships of black movements in the region became more visible.

In the context of globalization, a confluence of what could even be contradictory interests between states, major international organizations, ethnic movements, and other actors who participate in the interactions but which were produced as a result of recognition policies has been generated (Agudelo, Recondo 2007) and the affirmation of indigenous peoples' rights[9] has been strengthened along with their articulation of strategies to combat exclusion, poverty, environmental protection, and loss of biodiversity. The arguments circulating internationally on "democratic governability," the reduction in the size of the state and decentralization are associated with the need to give representation to new social interlocutors amongst which ethnic groups have a prominent place. As well as this, we should add discourses on sustainable development, the protection of biodiversity and environment, aspects in which these ethnic groups have become protagonists.

In the social sciences, there is renewed interest in the analysis of the processes of building historical and social identity amongst these populations. Going beyond the culturalist and historicist approaches, concepts such as *diaspora, hybrid, contextual and multiple identities* are consolidating themselves in order to account for the complexity of the problem faced by these populations and the societies in which they are immersed.[10] Academic discourse on the historical and contemporary trans-nationality of Afro-descendents will be another tool used by actors involved in the construction of black political mobilization in the region.

In this convergence of actors, discourses and policies, some of the front-line protagonists in the transformation of the public policies enforced in the countries of Latin America bring or increase the issue of the black populations in their discourses and action plans. Amongst them, we can mention the World Bank (IBRD), the Inter-American Development Bank (IDB), the United Nations (UN), the United Nations Development Program (UNDP), UNESCO, cooperation and development foundations, and NGOs.

Let us look at some examples from the texts of organizations like the Inter-American Development Bank and the World Bank:

> The representative of the Inter-American Development Bank has recommended evaluating, in the framework of the censuses and surveys amongst families, the situation of the indigenous and Afro-Latin American Peoples, using economic and social indicators as a basis. These indicators will give us a better idea about the poverty of these groups. He has also suggested involving civil society more, specially the NGOs, in projects and investing in the education of indigenous women and women of African origin, given the high number of illiterates amongst them and starting up programs to combat the violence and persecution to which these peoples are victim. (Extracts from the report of the "World Conference against Racism, Racial Discrimination, Xenophobia and Related Forms of Intolerance", Preparatory Committee, Second Session, Geneva, 21 May to 1 June, 2001)

In June, 2002, the IDB's Institute for Social Development gave a course on "social management" for twenty black Latin American leaders. The goals of the training organized were to learn how to implement projects and write reports, design strategies, negotiate, listen, resolve conflicts, write budgets and understand the decision making process. According to the IDB, "in order to get out of the vicious circle of exclusion (...) Afro-descendent leaders with the knowledge and training necessary to involve themselves in development programs and influence local and national political processes are required." The IDB bases its policies towards the black populations on its mission statement, "On social exclusion" (*www.iadb.org*).

As to the World Bank, its interest in black populations is presented as a product of the importance of the visibility process that operated during the years 1980-1990. There is an important statistical study that includes the racial variable in Brazil and other socio-demographic studies in countries such as Colombia, Peru and Ecuador. The World Bank was already insisting on "the fight against poverty" and was working on indigenous populations. The directive of this for indigenous peoples came into force in 1991, including the "race factor" as a mechanism of social exclusion.

The World Bank recognizes "the long abandonment of race related issues in Latin America by governments and interna-tional institutions" and the way "race, generalized poverty and social exclusion and income inequality are related..." (*www. bm.org*)

In the "Evaluación de los componentes de titulación colec-tiva de tierras a las comunidades indígenas y afrocolombianas del Pacífico, y de Comités Regionales del Plan de Manejo de Recursos Naturales (PMRN)" – August 1994 - the World Bank broadened its concept of indigenous peoples to include the black communities defined by Law 70 of 1993 (collective titling of lands for black communities). In this case, the World Bank's policy speaks of the articulation between ethnic groups and the environment. First, they are involved in the PMRN and then, as a mechanism to guarantee investment in the human groups found in the region. On the basis of this experience, sensitivity was shown towards the non-rural black populations through the policies against poverty.

Since June 2002, the World Bank has promoted work in part-nership with other institutions such as IDB, the Inter-American Foundation and Inter-American Dialogue (an agency derived from the IDB) creating the Inter-Agency Consultation on Race in Latin America. According to a report on an event on race and poverty organized by the World Bank, this consultation should become a "permanent instance, linking other institutions such as the Pan-American Health Organization (PAHO), the United Nations Development Program (UNDP), the Ford Foundation, and the Rockefeller Foundation, with the aim of "raising awareness within the international communities responsible for policies and development about problems faced by the peoples of African ancestry in Latin America and the Caribbean" (World Bank, Working Paper No.9 on Sustainable Development: Race and Poverty, 2002).

In 2006, Josefina Stubbs, a World Bank official, took part in CABO's strategic planning design workshop, a meeting that the World Bank had contributed to in Costa Rica. For Stubbs, CABO is "the only Network of Afro-descendents in the Americas that has worked uninterruptedly for more than 10 years for the rights of peoples and communities, for democracy and against racism and discrimination." She indicated that from her perspective as a World Bank official who works with Afro-descendents, "this is the best moment for the CABO to draw up a strategic plan, in order to face the great opportunities and challenges of putting the issues of Afro-descendents on the international agenda" (workshop on Strategic Plan of the CABO, X Anniversary, San José, Costa Rica, 2006 (Document, CABO Archives).

In the same meeting, Judith Morrison, the executive director of the Inter-Agency Consultation on Race in Latin America (IAC), attended and participated in a lecture on "Strategy and the international organizations." The IAC is considered by CABO as a "strategic ally." Morrison presented the components of the work of the IAC and the different organizations that make up this network, with respect to the Afro-descendent populations in Latin America. According to her lecture, improving the quality of statistical data (socio-economical data) on the Afro-descendent populations in Latin America and the Caribbean is one of the central objectives of the IAC aimed at designing more effective policies to confront the problems of these populations. For the IAC, there are three types of central interlocutors to their work: governments, other agencies, international authorities and social organizations. CABO assumes as one of its strategic orientations this work model as regards the influence with institutions and states, in particular the United States and Central American governments. The IAC considers the CABO as its main interlocutor amongst Central America's social organizations (Workshop on Strategic Plan, CABO Archives, 2006).

Finally, we will point out that another variant that contributed to create the conditions for the visibility and the transnational forms of political action of black movements in Latin America is the opposition that consolidated itself in the face of globalization, above all, with respect to its economic aspects (the entrenchment of the market and neo-liberalism). This rebellious activism was first known as an anti-globalization movement and is now vindicated more as "alterglobalization" in as far as it is recognized as an expression of the global context of exchanges and relations on planetary scale and vindicates the possibility of an "alternative globalism." The most visible sectors are made up by the different branches of the ecologist movement, like Greenpeace, organizations in *networks* like ATTC (Association for the Taxation of Financial Transactions and Citizen Action), PGA (Peoples' Global Action), Vía Campesina, and cultural and ethnic movements. Events like the Porto Alegre summit or the organization of large demonstrations and international meetings that confront the economic globalization driven by transnational financial institutions and other international instances show their great capacity for mobilization, their effects in the media, and their capacity for multiplication. Some Latin American black movements are linked to these processes and vindicate their participation in networks as part of their platform of struggle.

Emergence of the transnational networks

Amongst the elements that we have just presented as constituting the background of the emergence of transnational networks, the contacts and exchanges between leaders and representatives of black movements from different countries in Latin America will be presented, giving origin to initiatives for coordination and agreed political actions and explicitly demanded as *networks*. In each of these experiences, we will find that certain leaders play a key role and will be at the core of networks' organization. Prior to the formation of a network there are encounters and contacts in the framework of transnational seminars, forums and meetings dealing with racial, cultural, environmental, human rights or alterglobalist issues. These events are proposed by some of the national movements or the leaders who are promoting the idea of the network. They are also organized thanks to the initiative of international cooperation and development organizations and institutions such as those we have already mentioned. In the framework of these meetings, the networks are set up, generally on the initiative of the most important movements or those with most capacity to convene. The later co-opting of new members is done through established and regulated mechanisms.

The first experience we have knowledge of appears in 1992, being the Afro-Latin American and Caribbean Women's Network that emerged during the "First Encounter of Black Women", held in the Dominican Republic that same year. This organization emerges as an expression of the Latin American and Caribbean feminist movement, articulating demands of gender and race. This network was conceived as a space for coordinating initiatives to make visible the problems of black women on the issues of identity, discrimination, health, work and integration as well as being horizontal, democratic dynamics for political reflection and the drawing up of proposals. Representatives of Central American and Caribbean countries participated in the networks. The most visible leader of this process is the Afro-Costa Rican Epsy Campbell, a political, feminist community leader.

Two years later, in 1994, the "Continental Network of Afro-American Organizations" was set up on the initiative of Uruguay's black movement, Mundoafro, which promoted it during the first "Seminar against racism and xenophobia" held in Montevideo, Uruguay. Its strategic objective was the struggle against racism and discrimination by means of coordinated actions throughout the continent. We want to highlight here the explanation given by the organizers on the working principles that characterize a *network*:

1. Democratic relations between members.
2. A horizontal relationship.
3. Preservation of the autonomy and self-determination of the member organizations.
4. Dynamism in joint actions.
5. Openness to new members, discussion, proposals.

(Statutes, Mundoafro Archives, Montevideo, Uruguay, 1994)

Organizations from Honduras, Costa Rica, Peru, Colombia, Uruguay, Argentina, Paraguay, Brazil, Ecuador and the United States participated in this initiative. Romero Rodriguez is the most outstanding Afro-Uruguayan leader of this process.

In 1995, the Central American Black Organization (CABO) was founded in Dangriga (Belize) by of representatives from Honduras, Guatemala, Panama, Costa Rica, Nicaragua, Belize and organized communities of Afro-Central American migrants in the United States, mainly Garifuna. Amongst their strategic objectives and lines of action, they gave priority to the visibility of the problems facing the Afro-Central American peoples on an international scale and in their respective countries. In 2001, in the framework of the commitments established by the states in the Durban conference and the preparatory meeting in Santiago de Chile, CABO incorporated the resolutions of these meetings into their objectives. They also adhered to the Millennium Goals defined by the United Nations. Another point highlighted by CABO was the need to exert "influence" by means of a "lobbying" policy amongst other political and social actors in the United States that, in turn, could put pressure on the Central American governments to get them to respond to their claims. The strengthening of relations with the North American black movement and other movements in Latin America and the Caribbean also appeared amongst their priorities. CABO regularly visited the United States and maintained talks with a number of actors (NGOs, cooperation agencies, and international organizations, as well as government agencies) the most important of which are the IDB, the Ford Foundation, US-AID, the Black Caucus, black churches, and union organizations.

In addition to its membership in the Afro-Latin American and Caribbean Strategic Alliance, of which we will discuss later, since 2000 CABO has managed to become a member of the Consultative Council of the System for Central American Integration (CC-SICA),[11] to participate in the United Nations Commission on Sustainable Development and to become a participative member of the National Alliance of Latin American and Caribbean Communities (NALACC, USA).[12]

The ONECA's actions are coordinated from the city of La Ceiba, Honduras, in the same building as the ODECO (Organización de Desarrollo Comunitario), a Honduran movement and leading member and co-founder of the ONECA. The principal leader of the ODECO, Celeo Álvarez, is one of the most visible Afro-Latin American leaders in transnational spaces and has been a key figure in the running of CABO from its birth. Another leader who was also part of CABO's governing body is the Afro-Costa Rican leader, Epsy Campbell, highly recognized in the international sphere and today a high-ranking political figure in her own country as a leader of a national party.

The "Afroamérica XXI" network was formed in 1996, one year after the foundation of CABO. The context of its appearance was the elaboration of a study aimed at gathering information on the situation of black populations in various Latin American countries, as well as contacting black leaders to encourage the strengthening of already existing organizations and the formation of new ones where necessary. This project had the financial support of the IDB and the Canadian Cooperation Agency. In November 1996, the "Afroámerica XXI" project was launched during the "Forum on poverty and minorities in Latin America and the Caribbean" held in Washington. With the representation of 15 countries, the goals of this initiative are similar to those presented in the "Continental Network" in 1994 in Uruguay. The person at the core of the formation of Afroamérica XXI was the Afro-American-Jamaican, Michael Franklin. With the support of part of the IDB and other institutions in the United States, this organization initially had a great capacity for coordination and managed to group together most Latin American black movements, including some that belonged to CABO and the Network created two years earlier in Uruguay. In the year 2000, due to contradictions within Afroamérica XXI, the most important movements left in order to form a new network. This new initiative questioned what they claimed to be Franklin's dominating and despotic management. Afroamérica XXI later removed Franklin as director and has continued to exist until today, although, in a considerably weakened form.

In the year 2000, during one of a number of continental meetings in preparation for the "World Conference against Racism, Racial Discrimination, Xenophobia and Related Forms of Intolerance", the Afro-Latin American and Caribbean Strategic Alliance was formed in San José, Costa Rica and presented as its objectives:

1. Make visible the presence of the Afro-Latin American and Caribbean communities along with their organizations.
2. Ensure equality and access to all economic, social, political and cultural instances and resources.
3. Incorporate a gender as well as ethno-racial perspectives.
4. Favor the empowerment and full participation of the Afro-Latin American and Caribbean communities.

(Declaration of San José, Archives of the Strategic Alliance, Montevideo, Uruguay, 2000)

The Alliance is the expression of the contradictions within the continental black movement that got worse in the process of preparing for the Durban Conference. Michael Franklin became isolated from the majority of the region's movements. The leaders who promoted the Alliance initiative are Romero Rodríguez of Uruguay, Celeo Álvarez of Honduras, Epsy Campbell from Costa Rica, Edna Roland from Brazil, Jesús *Chucho* García of Venezuela and Carlos Rosero from Colombia. The objectives established by the Alliance are not fundamentally different from those outlined by earlier experiences. The context in which it emerges (preparation for the Durban Conference) is the moment of greatest visibility of the black movements in Latin America. This network is the most representative in the region. Until the year 2005, there are records of the activities organized by the Alliance. Since then, the priority given to national dynamics of the principal movements that form the Alliance has made its presence almost disappear even without its dissolution or new contradictions and differences between the member organizations.

Finally, since 2003, meetings of black congress members of the Americas began with the aim of building coordination mechanisms for their tasks defined as support and active participation in all the processes vindicating the rights of the populations of black origin on the continent. The first meeting was held in Brazil, 2003, the second in Bogotá in 2004, and the third in San José and Limón, Costa Rica, 2005. These meetings had the support of international organizations like the IDB, the UNDP, some national organizations of black populations and in certain occasions the help of parliaments of the respective countries. This network was formed on the initiative of a number of black parliamentarians from Brazil, Colombia, and Costa Rica. During the 2005 meeting in Costa Rica, in which members of congress of twenty-two countries of the continent participated (including Canada and the United States), was decided the creation the Black Parliament of the Americas that held its first meeting in Cali, Colombia, in 2006. One of the aspects criticized by the parliamentarians who have been involved in the process until now, is the political under-representation of the populations of African origin in the political institutions of the countries in the region.[13]

The form of action in networks is presented as the most effective way of coordinating the work of this group. "We urge the establishing of alliances with international organizations as well as our national, regional and local governments. In this way, we accumulate strength on the experience of the work of other networks instead of trying to substitute them..." (Final Declaration of the Parliamentary Encounter in Costa Rica, 2005). The leader and Costa Rican parliamentarian Epsy Campbell, along with other parliamentarians from Costa Rica, Colombia, Brazil and Canada made up the directorate.

Functioning of the networks:
Possibilities and limitations

Once the networks are constituted, we find in all cases similar modes of functioning. The communication mechanism between members executed via Internet, setting up virtual forums and discussions, e-mails, setting up webpages that provide access to documents, information, and in some cases provide possible interactivity (forums, sending opinions, debates, etc.) as well. It should be said that within each organization most members do not have access to these means of communication that can inable them to participate actively in the life of the network. As for direct contact, this is even more restricted to the leaders who have representation in the international space and assume the role of spokespersons for their organizations. In some cases, these same persons have been chosen by their movements to take on this role. On other occasions, the big international institutions (IAC, IDB, UNO, Unesco, etc) promote the events in which the members of the network establish contact. The institutions determine who is to attend by means of personal invitations. The international events are not organized with the sole aim of carrying out activities of the network. In most cases, meetings and encounters in which the issues related to the black populations are discussed are also used to organize parallel meetings of the networks' members attending. It is in this type of meeting that the networks have been formed.

The black movements do not have the economic resources available to finance autonomous transnational encounters and the different international institutions with which the movements interact provide key support in this sense. The main institutions have also adopted the network form as an association mechanism in order to intervene in the racial problem in Latin America. As we have already mentioned, in the year 2000, the IAC (Inter-Agency Consultation on Race in Latin America) emerged and constituted itself as the institution that has provided the most support for these transnational encounter spaces. The main participant institutions in the IAC are:

- World Bank
- Inter-American Development Bank
- Department of International Development of the United Kingdom
- Pan-American Health Organization
- Ford Foundation
- Inter-American Foundation
- Human Rights Commission of Organization of American States
- Inter-American Dialogue (an IDB organization) that serves as secretariat for the IAC.

The leaders of the movements that participate in international events are essential to the functioning of the networks, but there is a certain hierarchy within them. Greater leadership and visibility is the benefit for those who manage the initiatives or those who have more relations and capacity for dialogue with the institutions that support them or more facility to travel to the centers where decisions are taken on the organization of events or financial help. The representatives in the international arenas are not only leaders recognized by their respective movements but also have cultural capital that facilitates their role as interlocutors in this environment. In the cases studied, they are professional intellectuals, with work experience in consulting activities and other contractual forms with national and international organizations in issues related to their demands.

We can also observe a certain hierarchical location of the spaces in which the networks are active. In this sense, the poles where the activity is concentrated are cities such as Washington, the venue of the IAC offices (and of its main participants) and Geneva, the headquarters of the United Nations Human Rights Commission and the meeting place of the Working Group on Peoples of African Descent, that emerged as a result of the Durban Conference. The networks often assume a bilateral form of relations: on the one hand between the leaders representing their movements and specific local and national interests and on the other, an international agency with which a project is carried while the relation with other members of the network falls into second place.

An aspect in which the flexibility of participation in the network is evident is the autonomy of the member organizations. Depending on local priorities, each group decides on its degree of participation in a determined initiative. Members can disappear from the network for periods and then integrate themselves again depending on their availability. This is what has happened to the Strategic Alliance since 2005. When speaking to one of its most important leaders, Romero Rodríguez of Mundafro, in Uruguay in 2007, he declared that the Alliance has entered a period of "hibernation" from the alliance in which each organization has had to concentrate on their national agendas but that in any moment, when the situation permits it, they will reactivate themselves again.

For the black movements it is very important to maintain a discourse on belonging to a community in the transnational sense (the Black Diaspora, their common history, their African descent, being victims of racism and discrimination, etc.) as a factor of legitimacy and reinforcement of the vindications in their local and national spaces. However, we can observe that action in the transnational networks occurs in function with interests established from the "inside." Priority is given to participation in networks to the extent that they contribute to strengthening the political projects of each group on the national scene in any given moment. In any case, we should not forget the increasingly frequent overlapping between the national and transnational scene that mean that even the most local demands (territorial, for economic, social or political rights etc.), can nourish the arenas of transnational struggle giving legitimacy to the movements and their spokesmen as representatives of "tangible" causes.

Conclusions

On the basis of this still incomplete overview of the organizational forms assumed by the black movements on a transnational scale that vindicate themselves as *networks*, we can conclude that they are forms of action and organization with a low degree of formalization that gather these movements together with a changeable degree of intensity according to factors that determine the priority and intensity of the action. This definition fits well with the synthesis posed by Colonomos (1995) and equally with the classic reference of Granovetter (197) on the effectiveness of the "weak ties." While it is true that we do not find a clear hierarchical and vertical structure, the horizontal nature of the social relations normally attributed to networks does not apply in most of the cases we have observed. There is a correlation of forces within the networks, some localized spaces of power from which the network acquires meaning and also certain disequilibrium in access to the symbolic resources, and to the social capital that determines who is best located on the scale of relations inside the networks.

These interactions within the transnational space acquire a determining role as an effective form of action. We have seen how, on the level of discourse, the symbols of belonging to a community that goes far beyond national frontiers are articulated. This community of meaning and history becomes a central element of the discourses of the black movement and also an instrumental tool in local struggles as a factor of legitimacy.

According to our level of observation, the networks are not an end in themselves, but instead a form of interaction that is used by the movements they belong to according to their priorities of "accumulation of forces." The networks that we have studied can appear and disappear according to the specific conditions of the context in which they and theirs members act. They are not actors in themselves, or bearers of identity just because they imply a specific form of relation but rather due to the discourses, the representations and actions that can be articulated within them.

For the Latin American black movements and the case of the CABO in Central America we can see that the so-called networks have responded to their needs for interaction in a world in which their visibility has been constructed through the dynamic articulation of local, national and international rationales.

Table 3.1: Presence of leaders in International meetings (based on 35 meetings between 1992 and 2005)

NAME	COUNTRY	ORGANIZATION	%
Romero Rodríguez	Uruguay	Mundo Afro Coordinator Strategic Alliance	56%
Epsy Campbell	Costa Rica	Partido de Acción Ciudadana CABO (Organización Negra Centramericana) Stategic Alliance	42%
Carlos Rosero	Colombia	PCN (Proceso de Comunidades Negras) Strategic Alliance	39%
Jesús *Chucho* García	Venezuela	Fundación Afroamercia Strategic Alliance	39%
Edna Roland	Brazil	Fala Preta Geledés Strategic Alliance	21%
Michael Franklin	United States	OOA (Organization of Africans in the Americas) Afroamerica XXI	12%

Notes

1. Text based on the article "Les réseaux transnationaux comme forme d'action dans les mouvements noirs d'Amérique latine". *Cahiers des Amériques latines.* 51-52, 2006. Translated by Susan L. Jones Harris.

2. In the island nations of the Caribbean, where there is a majority Afro-descendent population, racial problems and those linked with identity have specific historical and contemporary characteristics to which we will not refer in this text.

3. Extract from the conclusions of the Workshops on Strategic Plan for CABO, X Anniversary, San Juan, Costa Rica, 2006 (Document: CABO Archives)

4. See the encyclopedic work of Manuel Castels (1996).

5.   In particular, my doctoral dissertation "Populations noires et participation politique dans le Pacifique colombien: Les paradoxes d'une inclusion ambigue", directed by Christian Gros IHEAL, Paris, 2002.

6.   There is a very rich and diverse bibliography on this point. On indigenous mobilization in the context of globalization, see (Bellier, Legros 2001).

7.   An excellent compendium of Works on the Garifuna can be found in (Palacio 2005).

8.   For Colombia there is the case of the Palenque de San Basilio on the Caribbean Coast, near the city of Cartagena, and their leader Benkos Bioho.

9.   Although the black populations are not considered as indigenous, there is an association with their character as groups culturally differentiated and submitted, in the same way as the indigenous ones, to racial discrimination, exclusion and with no recognition of their cultural features.

10. The concept of Diaspora is discussed by Hall (1994) and Gilroy (1993). This category is criticized by Chivallon (2004). A bibliographical revision of recent trends in studies on ethnicity can be consulted in Agudelo (2005b).

11. This is an official body for the process of Central American integration; CABO participates actively in the part corresponding to the Permanent Civil Society Forum of the Central American Commission on Environment and Development of the Central American Integration System.

12. This is a coordinator of non-governmental organizations that defends Latin American and Caribbean immigrant's rights in the United States.

13. We do not have statistics available on the number of black parliamentarians in Latin America, but in the countries where the political mobilization of these groups is most visible (for example, Brazil, Costa Rica) there is repeated denunciation of the absence of adequate democratic mechanisms for participation and representation of the black populations. See Agudelo (2005b).

Bibliography

Agudelo, Carlos. 2002. *Populations noires et participation politique dans le Pacifique colombien: Les paradoxes d'une inclusion ambiguë*, doctoral dissertation directed by C. Gros. Paris: IHEAL- Université Paris III La Sorbonne Nouvelle.

Agudelo, Carlos. 2005a. Le comportement électoral des populations noires en Amérique latine. Un regard à partir du cas colombien. In *Voter dans les Amériques*, eds. Jean-Michel Blanquer et al. Paris: Editions de l'Institut des Amériques, IHEAL, Paris III.

Agudelo, Carlos. 2005b. *Retos del multiculturalismo en Colombia. Política y poblaciones negras*. Medellín: La Carreta, IEPRI-IRD-ICANH.

Agudelo, Carlos. 2006. Les réseaux transnationaux comme forme d'action chez les mouvements noirs d'Amérique latine. *Cahiers de l'Amérique latine* 51-52.

Agudelo, Carlos y David Recondo. 2007. Multiculturalismo en América latina. Del Pacífico mexicano al Pacífico colombiano. In *Los retos de la diferencia. Los actores de la multiculturalidad entre México y Colombia*, eds. Odile Hoffmann y María Teresa Rodríguez. México: CIESAS, IRD, ICANH, CEMCA.

Bellier, Irène y Dominique Legros. 2001. Mondialisation et redéploiement des pratiques politiques amérindiennes. Esquisses théoriques. *Recherches amérindiennes au Québec*, XXXI(3).

Castels, Manuel. 1996. *The Rise of the Network Society*. Oxford: Blackwell Publishers.

Chivallon, Christine. 2004. *La diaspora noire des Amériques. Expériences et théories à partir de la Caraïbe*. Paris: CNRS Editions.

Colonomos, Ariel. 1995. *Sociologie des réseaux transnationaux. Communautés, entreprises et individus : lien social et système international*. Paris: L'Harmattan.

Gilroy, Paul. 1993. *The black Atlantic: modernity and double consciousness*. London: Verso.

Granovetter, Mark. 1973. The strength of weak ties. *American Journal of Sociology* 78(7): 1360-1380.

Gros, Christian. 1997. *Pour une sociologie des populations indiennes et paysannes de l'Amérique latine*. Paris: L'Harmattan.

Hall, Stuart. 1994 [1990]. Cultural identity and Diaspora. In *Colonial Discourse and Post-Colonial Theory. A. Reader* eds P. Williams, L Chrismas. London: Harsvester-Wheatsheaf.

Mercklé, Pierre. 2004. *Sociologie des réseaux sociaux*. Paris: La Découverte.

Palacio, Joseph. 2005. *The Garifuna a nation across borders. Essays in Social Anthropology*. Belize: Editorial Cubola,

Sansone, Livio. 1998. Negritudes et racismes globais? Uma tentativa de relativizar alguns dos novos paradigmas «Universais» nos estudos da etnicidade a parir da realidade brasileira. *Horizontes antropologicos* 8: 227-237.

Sansone, Livio. 2000. Os objetos da identidade negra: consumo, mercantilizaçao, globalizaçao e criaçao de culturas negras no Brasil. *Mana* 6(1): 87-120.

Wade, Peter. 1999. La population noire en Amérique latine: multiculturalisme, législation et situation territoriale. *Problèmes d'Amérique latine* 32: 3-16.

Wade, Peter. 1993. *Blackness and Race Mixture: The Dynamics of Racial Identity in Colombia*. Baltimore: Johns Hopkins University Press.

Wade, Peter. 1997. *Race and ethnicity in Latin America*. London: Pluto Press.

Chapter 4

THE RENAISSANCE OF AFRO-MEXICAN STUDIES[1]

Odile Hoffmann

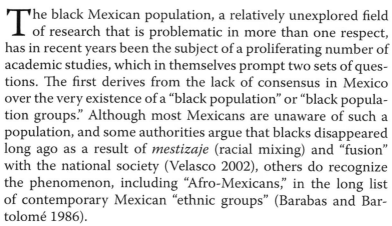

The black Mexican population, a relatively unexplored field of research that is problematic in more than one respect, has in recent years been the subject of a proliferating number of academic studies, which in themselves prompt two sets of questions. The first derives from the lack of consensus in Mexico over the very existence of a "black population" or "black population groups." Although most Mexicans are unaware of such a population, and some authorities argue that blacks disappeared long ago as a result of *mestizaje* (racial mixing) and "fusion" with the national society (Velasco 2002), others do recognize the phenomenon, including "Afro-Mexicans," in the long list of contemporary Mexican "ethnic groups" (Barabas and Bartolomé 1986).

Debate on this subject resembles a dialogue of the deaf, so poorly delineated are its terms; both sides seek to recognize, for opposite reasons, an established "ethnic group" that can be defined by objectively describable "cultural" traits distinct from those of "others," generally identified as whites or Indians. Notable here is an essentialist tendency widely criticized in anthropology and relatively easy to challenge, since "cultural characteristics" can be borrowed and transformed, acquiring meaning only in given historical and sociopolitical configurations, through the actions and interactions of coexisting social protagonists. The authors cited above themselves espouse a "procedural" model and seek to record "realities" insofar as the group adopts certain specific collective descriptors for itself (Barabas and Bartolomé 1986), occasionally invoking a strategic essentialism needed for political-ethnic negotiation and mobilization.

The question remains as to whether, in the Mexican context, a "black identity" or specifically "black" characteristics can reasonably be cited to explain more general social processes; and if so, why and for whom? How, where, and when might this "identity" be expressed, and what does it cover? The instrumentalist approach to identity (Glazer and Moynihan 1975) is unsatisfactory here, since Mexico has no external, institutionalized categorization that recognizes the "black identity" and associates it with specific measures or material, political or cultural advantages. Thus, any expression of or claim to black identity should be understood independently of any identity strategy directly linked to multicultural policies or power relations between established "communities."

A possible alternative to the radically essentialist and instrumentalist options might be a middle course that, clearly situated within a constructivist perspective, takes advantage of the life experience of those involved in order to understand the processes of identity construction "from the inside" – rather than the margins – of that group constituted by people claiming to be "different" because they are "black" (rarely)[2] or, more commonly, "*morenos*" (brown or dark-skinned). This is concordant with the ideas put forward by Hal Levine, who, although recognizing the impact of external categorizations, seeks to rehabilitate a vision of ethnicity that comes from within the group. He defines ethnicity minimalistically as "that method of classifying people (both self and other) that uses origin (socially constructed) as its primary reference" (Levine 1999, 168). The classification of people by their origins determines the boundaries as well as the contents of the groups thus catalogued, and both processes are equally important. Although in recent times anthropology has stressed boundaries over content, we must also consider the mechanisms by which the people themselves signify ("fill up") these categories (Levine 1999, 171). Barth himself, returning to the subject of his famous 1969 article, has clarified that it is not enough to analyze boundary processes, and that "central and culturally valued institutions and activities in an ethnic group may be deeply involved in its boundary maintenance by setting internal processes of convergence into motion" (Barth 1994, 11-32). Ethnicity is thus a process and result of categorization – a categorization that is constantly being revised to reflect the contexts and spaces in which it takes place. If we apply these few analytical principles, the case of the Afro-Mexicans is particularly interesting since the categorization of this group is still a fluid work in progress, in contrast to Latin-American countries such as Colombia, for example, where the existence of a "black ethnic group" is no longer disputed (even if the group's boundaries and content are and should be open to discussion).

In Mexico, we must begin by wondering whether the concept of "ethnicity" is the best way of accounting for the current dynamics of identity, and what agents and discourses are driving this orientation. The fact is that the local Afro-Mexican populations seem less interested in defining their "ethnic status" than in denouncing the discrimination against them and in demanding acknowledgement of their "Mexican" identity, which is often challenged (Lewis 2000). Their claim to difference can be interpreted in terms of collective rather than ethnic identity. As Wachtel has noted in a different context (Andean communities), "you can't see ethnicity everywhere," and we must avoid confusing ideas that, under the common rubric of "identity," are in fact dealing with separate questions (Wachtel 1992. On this confusion, see also Wieviorka 2004).

The intersection of these questions – ethnic identity and collective identity, the endogenous and exogenous dimensions of identity – necessarily involves analyzing the spaces where the processes of identity construction are forged and revealed. In this context space is understood in both its senses: as a scale or level of identity expression (individual, group or collective), and as a concrete geographical place around which identification is organized. This is not the same thing as identifying oneself as "black" to the neighbour or the researcher, or the same as doing so in the village, or in a neighbouring village in the same region, let alone in the capital. Any analysis of the contexts (particularly institutional ones) in which identity is expressed must therefore take that spatial dimension into account – an approach that may help us clarify, for example, the relations between collective identity and ethnic identity, or between identity and territory.

My second set of questions concerns the manner in which research on this subject is conducted today and how it has been conducted in the past. An examination of the "pedigree" of specialized studies in this field will clarify the antecedents and interpretative trends that have left their mark on current issues, explain their strong and weak points, and, ultimately, suggest some avenues of research.

These two sets of questions obviously overlap. My aim here, in reviewing the literature, is to approach the more theoretical and methodological questions while not losing sight of my double objective, namely, to determine the current status of Afro-Mexican studies within the context of intellectual discourse on black populations, and to decide how analysis of this "social group" should be approached. This article is divided into three parts. The first establishes the context of the issues involved in Afro-Mexican identity. The second part traces the history of research on the subject, pointing out a strong tendency to essentialization, while the third part analyzes the agents of today's ethnicization. In conclusion, I will explore some possible avenues of research.

The Black Population of Mexico: The Missing Link?

The existence and importance of the black populations on the Latin-American subcontinent are no longer topics confined to specialized academic circles; these populations are the subject of wide-ranging national and international debates, in political as well as academic forums. "Afrodescendants," a term used since the International Conference against Racism, Racial Discrimination, Xenophobia and Related Intolerance (Durban, 2001) by black organizations to distinguish themselves from the African Americans of the United States, are recognized as "ethnic communities" in the constitutions of several countries that are laying down specific measures designed to combat discrimination and promote an integration that recognizes individual differences (in Colombia, for example[3]).

Mexico comes to these debates from a singular position. Although the Mexican state recognized the country's multi-ethnic and multicultural nature in the constitutional reform of 1992, no executive law ever followed. The political options ratified by the country in the 1990s (adherence to the Organization of Economic Cooperation and Development, the North American Free Trade Agreement with Canada and the United States) hamper its ability to frame laws benefiting specific groups, primarily the Indians,[4] since such laws would contravene the principle of free circulation of goods and services (Hoffmann 2001). Despite political mobilization, social demands, protests, and the neo-Zapatista insurrection of 1994, the political ambiguities have not yet been resolved, and the multiculturalism trumpeted at the federal level is not reflected in any concrete measures.

With respect to the black population, or "population of African origin," the Mexican attitude is even more ambiguous. Although in most of the country the magnitude of slavery and of the black presence in history is a confirmed and well-documented fact, the same does not apply to contemporary black populations, whose existence as individuals and, especially, as a social group is not recognized by any legal document. Nevertheless, the cultural institutions, certain researchers, and some militants for the black cause – not necessarily operating from the same perspective – are helping to construct a new field of study or interpretation concerning the black population in Mexico. I would here like to explore the ins and outs of this recent intellectual and political construction, this "renaissance" of Afro-Mexican studies,[5] by putting it in its institutional, political, and social context.

Some strong hypotheses guide this analysis. The first one has already been widely confirmed – namely, that in Mexico the identity spectrum is entirely taken up by national identity on one hand and the Indian identities on the other.[6] The two identities – the national identity symbolizing the country's unity and the indigenous identities legitimizing and organizing cultural diversity – are integrated by the discourse of *mestizaje*, which is not new; it has been around since the end of the nineteenth century and was revived after the Revolution of 1910-1920. The emergence of other identity claims must, in this context, come under the heading of either exception or exoticism, applicable to populations of very specific origins (the Chinese who arrived from the Philippines in the seventeenth century, the Japanese forced labour, or, more recently, the Moslems, Koreans, and others). For a long time, studies on black populations were forced into this mould, making the "black" inhabitant a purely historical and extinct figure.

With the renewal of interest in contemporary black populations, the question arises as to what conceptual framework should be adopted. This brings me to my second hypothesis: the black population's historical development makes Mexico a unique case in Latin America, to which the most modern interpretations can be applied only with difficulty. This would partially explain the relatively impoverished theoretical basis of research in this field, but it could also become a powerful impetus if the dynamism of such studies continues and grows.

Unlike other Latin-American countries, Mexico has no social movement of black identity that might justify analytical approaches based on social and political movements (Touraine 1988). The population in question is numerically very small (a few tens of thousands, out of Mexico's 100 million inhabitants in 2000) and politically non-existent. It displays no cultural or religious practices indicative of an "Afro identity" that could be mobilized for political purposes, as might be the case in Brazil or Cuba (Argyriadis and Capone 2004). Nor are there any specific measures (except for a few exceptions referred to below) around which the demands of "black" groups or collectives could be organized, a situation that militates against the now classic interpretations of identity construction and instrumentalization: there is objectively no advantage – political, ideological, or material – in "being" (becoming, claiming to be) black. If there is any construction, it will come from elsewhere. Neither the official discourse nor those political actors with national influence have any specific way of referring to the populations that define themselves as *"morenos"* or *"afromestizos."*

At the same time, postmodern reflections on the invention of identity and individuals' capacity for negotiating their multiple identities in the context of relationships and situations (Hall 1994) run aground on the fact that these identities can only be expressed where there are legitimizing frameworks—precisely what "black" Mexicans lack, since they have no place on the national identity chessboard. With no possibility of dialogue with some "other" who would recognize their own alterity, and particularly not with the state, Afro-Mexicans have no border they could cross to integrate into another available identity category (Indians, *mestizos*, whites). They remain in a kind of limbo that they accept as *"afromestizos"* or *"morenos"* or, most often, as "Mexicans" (Lewis 2000)—that is, in either case, outside the prevailing ethnic categorizations.

However, at both extremes of the social space, contexts still exist where "being black" may become a relevant part of social dynamics. At the local level, where differences are negotiated day to day with or without an explicit conceptual system, *"morenos"* suffer racism and discrimination from their non-black neighbours in the most trivial as well as the most complex acts and words (Castillo Gómez 2000). This shared experience of routine racism is the surest way to cement an "identity." or at the very least an alterity that is constantly brought up by those around them.[7] This can then give rise to all kinds of individual strategies for evading the stigma (negation/denial), reversing it (affirmation) or ignoring it (avoidance). The approaches to human interaction developed by Erving Goffman, used notably by Cunin in similar contexts in Colombia (Cunin 2004), can help us understand the ambiguities and contradictions that often characterize the identity positions taken by *afromestizos* – ambiguities that preclude any talk of an obvious or "natural" identity but that nevertheless always bring into play the "racial" dimension of difference.

At the other end of the social space, international forums propose their own operational categories for thinking about black identity. The networks of Afro militants, the specialized international agencies against racism, and the United Nations documents on slavery all offer legitimate sources of categorizations that do not exist at the national level. One recent conceptualization is the diaspora, a model that its proponents say is warranted by the traumatic original de-territorialization and subsequent dispersion of slaves to the four corners of the earth, mainly America. There is no consensus on this, however. What are the common myths that would give coherence to a supposed "black diaspora"? What are its instruments (rituals, for example) and modes of expression? Without entering into this debate, let us simply say that most American black or *afromestizo* societies do not share this globalized arena but are anchored instead in extremely localized and territorialized realities, grappling with alliances and rivalries that affect their material and spiritual survival. The door does remain open for a handful of activists who, although a minority, exert remarkable influence over collective representations through their participation in debates and international mobilization. For the time being, however, the diaspora concept remains largely alien to the Afro-Mexican population and cannot be said to provide a truly operational theoretical framework.

This rapid overview of the current situation of Afro-Mexicans offers a few useful points of reference for the rest of our argument: Mexico is apparently the "missing link" in Latin America. The term was coined by a black activist who was expressing his view that Mexico's unique character (its absence of both any black ethnic movement and any conventional ethnic categorization, whether endogenic or exogenic) in fact excluded it from the collective agenda adopted by the international Afro networks. However, both the micro and macro levels present a number of sources of "black" identification that could be mobilized for some future ethnogenesis. Although it may be presumptuous today to speak of a "black ethnicity" in

Mexico, it is impossible to deny the experience of alterity and expressions of collective identity assumed by the *afromestizos.*

The specifics of the contemporary Mexican situation derive in large part from the way the black population established itself in the country. In Mexico, like everywhere else in Latin America, the black inhabitants are the descendants of individuals brought to the country as slaves. These slaves were employed in many sectors, sometimes concentrated by region (mines, sugar-cane plantations, cattle ranches), but more often scattered in both cities (crafts, domestic service, manual labour) and rural areas, virtually all over the country (Martínez Montiel 1994). During the colonial period, they lived through the classic, dramatic history of resistances, revolts, escapes, and the establishment of *palenques* (communities of free blacks and escaped slaves),[8] especially in plantation regions such as Veracruz, where slavery persisted until the nineteenth century (Naveda Chávez-Hita 1987, Caroll 1991). Elsewhere, from the beginning of the eighteenth century, as the Indian population began to grow again, the influx of slaves dwindled (Aguirre Beltrán 1972, 85) and black *mestizaje* increased, particularly – although not exclusively – with the Indians, with whom the Afro-Mexicans shared their subjugation to the Spanish, creoles, and *mestizos.* The main consequences of this "early" termination of black slave importation were an intensified rate of *mestizaje* and a rapid decline in the percentage of slaves in the black population, two characteristics that set the black population of Mexico apart from those of other Latin American countries.[9] At the time that slavery was outlawed (first prohibited in 1810, it was abolished in 1817, but the final decree of abolition was signed by Vicente Guerrero only in 1829[10]), the black populations (described as *negros, pardos y mulatos* in the censuses) of Mexico were already largely of mixed race, comprising peasants, labourers, and "free" artisans (one option for the poor classes of the eighteenth century, although they were usually subject to harsh mechanisms of bossist, clientelistic, or paternalistic rule).[11]

However, these trends were unequally distributed, and gave rise to distinct socio-geographic systems. In certain regions where hybridization was delayed and the proportion of blacks was higher, different regional identities have integrated, evoking the population's black origins without being limited to them: *jarochos* in Veracruz, *guaches* in the warm lands of Morelia, *mascogos* in Coahuila. In other places black phenotypes (skin colour, hair type) may be common without having given rise to any distinctive identity constructions. The only exception is the Pacific coast of Guerrero-Oaxaca (Costa Chica), a "multi-ethnic" region where groups of self-identified Indians, *morenos*, and *mestizos* live in proximity.[12] The total population comes to several tens of thousands of people (unlike the Indians, the black population is not the subject of a specific census). This is the region where the main claims of black identity in Mexico today are expressed and studied. It is also the place where the first ethnographic study on the black populations in Mexico was carried out (Aguirre Beltrán 1989).

The Scientific and Institutional Framework

Research Pedigree

The father of Afro-Mexican studies is unquestionably Gonzálo Aguirre Beltrán. A physician by training, Aguirre Beltrán was already an established anthropologist when, in 1942, Manuel Gamio, head of the Demography Department in the Interior Ministry, commissioned him to conduct a study on the black population in Mexico. This was the beginning of a remarkable historical project that, using archival sources, for the first time meticulously traced the origins and extent of the slave trade, the rates at which slaves arrived, their distribution in the country, the sectors of slave activity, and the process of *mestizaje*; conclusions were also drawn concerning the magnitude of the contribution that the populations of African origin had made to Mexican culture and history (Aguirre Beltrán 1972).

A few years later, following a visit to the US, where he studied with Melville Herskovits, Gonzálo Aguirre Beltrán carried out his first ethnographic study, in the village of Cuajinicuilapa on the coast of Guerrero (published in 1958). At the time still geographically isolated (the Pan-American Highway was not built until the 1960s) and inhabited mainly by populations of largely unmixed race, the Costa Chica seemed the last preserve of a black population that was gradually disappearing through racial intermixing. The reason Aguirre Beltrán spoke of "blacks" and forged the concept of "*afromestizos*" in this connection[13] was to better underline their exceptional nature and to reaffirm his thesis on the integration of "blacks and their mixtures" (*negros y sus mezclas*) in Mexican national society.[14]

In this view, integration was founded historically on two processes that differentiated blacks from other subordinate groups, in this case the Indians. For one, the cultural characteristics of the black population were not considered sufficiently distinctive to serve as criteria of ethnic identification; at the same time, their racial characteristics disappeared rapidly as a result of repeated *mestizaje*. At the end of the colonial period, it was not possible to base severe discrimination (*incapacidades asignadas*) on these tenuous differences. One by-product of this was that there was no solid support for forming or maintaining separate groups for the black and mulatto populations (Aguirre Beltrán 1972, 287). In contrast, the caste system of colonial society assigned a subordinate but recognized status to the Indians, who continued to live in a separate world during the early days of national independence. In contrast, the *afromestizo* and *mestizo* populations, unrecognized by the colonial system, were to become the foundation of a new independent system that, aspiring to a "national" population base, needed these masses, which although previously marginalized did not form a clearly separate caste (Aguirre Beltrán 1972, 291). Thus, Aguirre Beltrán theorized, political-structural mechanisms – the need to integrate the working classes in order to create a post-colonial "national society" – and socio-cultural mechanisms – the mixture of racial and cultural traits – converged to promote an almost complete integration of the black and mulatto populations into the national population and their consequent disappearance as a specific group within contemporary society. It should be noted that in his analyses, Aguirre Beltrán maintained that for both blacks and Indians ethnic differences were created and transformed through power relations.

Although this anti-essentialist approach was before its time, it was not emulated or even noticed for many years.

This theory of integration was so popular that for a long time it blocked any study of contemporary black populations, which were considered "not really authentic" and in any case were fated to disappear very quickly. It should be mentioned that during the same period (1940-1960), Mexican anthropology was focusing on the study of Indian groups, being doubly influenced by indigenist public policy[15] and the theoretical and methodological development fostered by several Mexican and foreign researchers who established national anthropological thinking on the basis of case studies undertaken in Indian regions.[16]

This lack of legitimacy, which still weighs on Afro-Mexicanist ethnography today, had less of an impact on the field of historical research, which continued to develop and expand. Studies in this area are carried out today in many provincial universities:[17] the Colegio de México,[18] the Mora Institute,[19] and, particularly, the Instituto Nacional de Antropología e Historia (INAH—National Institute of Anthropology and History), with its specialized seminar on "Studies of Populations of African Origin." The terms used in these studies explicitly refer to the past, confining the research subjects strictly to their identity of origin: enslaved and definitively "other." The studies detail the regional conditions of slavery (Palmer Colin 1993, Naveda Chávez-Hita 1995, Guevera Sanginés 1994, Herrera Casasús 1994), but devote equal attention to the ways of life of certain groups (black women in Mexico, Velázquez Gutiérrez 1994), beliefs (studies on the Inquisition[20]), and, in general, "Afro-American culture's" contribution to the national culture.[21] In any case, interest in the historical view of the black populations has never waned, any more than interest in "folklore" studies (music, dance, oral tradition. Gutiérrez Avila 1988), on which Gabriel Moedano is the best-known expert (Moedano Navarro 1997).

In anthropology, however, the pioneering research of Gonzálo Aguirre Beltrán in black ethnography did not gain widespread acceptance, whereas the rest of his work strongly influenced the discipline, primarily valued for its theoretical and thematic innovation. As an administrator of the Instituto Nacional Indigenista and later the CIESAS (Centro de Investigacions y Estudios Superiores en Antropología Social), he himself assumed a leading role in the development of Mexican anthropology. However, it was only in the 1980s that another renowned anthropologist, Guillermo Bonfil Batalla, gave new impetus to ethnographical research by creating the programme "The Third Root" (*la Tercera Raíz*) in the Dirección General de Culturas Populares (DGCP—General Directorate of Popular Culture, today part of the Consejo Nacional para la Cultura y las Artes, or Conaculta). Directed by Luz María Martínez Montiel,[22] the programme recognizes the contribution made by populations of African origin to national culture (dance, music, food, oral literature), generating many specialized studies and publications on these topics and initiating national and international gatherings, as well as occasionally innovative debates. Not only does it lend legitimacy to the ethnographic approach in the scientific and institutional spheres, but even more importantly, it places this field of research in an international framework. In this respect, in fact, Mexico participates in the UNESCO programme entitled "The Slave Route," which for the last decade or so has promoted conferences and joint publications among African and Latin-American countries. Mexico's representative was Luz María Martínez Montiel, while Colombia's was Jaime Arocha, both anthropologists who in their respective countries represent the revival of contemporary Afro-Americanist studies and who promote a focus on the "African roots" of Latin-American black cultures.

The specialized works in this field can no longer be overlooked. Even though all articles invariably begin by complaining about the lack of previous research, such works do indeed exist. Although not very accessible, often highly biased, sometimes badly documented, and certainly much less numerous than those dealing with the Indian populations, they nevertheless constitute a significant body of work. A first bibliographic review by G. Moedano and a work in progress by Cristina Díaz based on her 1994 thesis (Moedano Navarro 1992, Díaz Pérez 1994) list some thousand titles, and master's and doctoral theses in anthropology are increasingly numerous, indicating a real interest in the subject on the part of students and their teachers.

The 1990s marked a true rise in the evolution of Afro-Mexicanist studies, which previously had been virtually limited to historical and cultural research. However, the current ethnographical approaches still show some weaknesses, attributable in part to their history.

The Afrogenetic Temptation and the Impossibility of Definition

The Afro-Mexicanist movement has not so far managed to throw off its nominalist compulsion to begin every discussion by establishing "who we are talking about" in terms of ethnic affiliation. In the second edition of their compendium *Etnicidad y pluralismo cultural. La dinámica étnica en Oaxaca*, Barabas and Bartolomé include "Afro-Mexicans" among the "17 ethnic groups of Oaxaca" (Barabas and Bartolomé 1986). This categorization is possible mainly because the state of Oaxaca has legislation that recognizes, institutes, and regulates ethnic difference. In the electoral domain, particularly, the laws validate mayoral election according to "habits and customs," which may vary from one municipality to the next (raised-hand vote, appointment by the council of elders, with or without participation by women and "foreigners" in the village, and so on).[23] The already established and institutionally recognized "ethnic system" is thus the easiest to adapt to the black populations. However, there is no apparatus for estimating and statistically describing the *"afromestizo* ethnic group," in contrast to the neighbouring Indian groups. The classic indicators normally used in Mexico do not work (language, clothing, "traditional" social organization), and each author concocts his or her own, usually based on common-sense criteria specific to the situation under study. Researchers end up adopting the categories used by those around them, usually without devoting any deep critical thought to them beforehand, a tendency that poses the risk of repeating and transmitting the stereotypes of difference – or indifference. Thus it is that "the *negro*" is considered to be in violent confrontation with the Indian in the Costa Chica area, a recurrent view[24] (among others) to this day, and one which – particularly through the use of the singular "the *negro*" – well reflects the stereotypical nature of these portrayals.

The fact is that no one can agree on the definition of *afromestizos* as an "ethnic group," much less its possible boundaries. The latter are constantly renegotiated according to the fluctuating contexts of alterity, and vary from one locality to the next, from one timeframe to the next, according to the political, economic, or social alliances and tensions of the moment. The Barthian model is useful for pinpointing these boundary movements, but it is ineffective for "defining" ethnic groups, a purpose for which it was not conceived (Barth 1981). An interpretation model based on "inter-ethnic relations," on the other hand, can only function – with difficulty – on the basis of monographs, which is the sole means of describing how differences are created and interpreted locally: differences between blacks and Indians in one place, between whites and Afro-Indians in another, between the three coexisting groups in yet another, and so on (Cervantes Delgado 1984). Obviously, however, the validity of such an approach declines in direct proportion to the degree of generalization or theorization it seeks to support. It is impossible to conceive of "the inter-ethnic" without first isolating separate "ethnic groups," a mission that is still at the very heart of the debates and polemics. It is here that the theoretical impasse blocking many researchers shows most clearly: as long as Mexican anthropology strives to define the boundaries of a potential "*afromestizo* (or Afro-Mexican) group," it will be incapable of grasping the processes by which this social entity is continually constructed and deconstructed – an entity that, although volatile and uncertain, is nevertheless active in the social field.

The ethnographical approach, which could avoid this bias and move its focus away from the ethnicization problem, sometimes plunges into it headlong. It should be added that this is usually the act of beginning anthropology students, who invest the necessary observation time and report on their work in well- or not-so-well-documented and rarely published university theses. Most of them cite the works of Aguirre Beltrán, whose ethnographic descriptions (written, it should be recalled, more than half a century ago) emphasized the traces of Africanity in the way his subjects walked, built houses, or carried babies, for example, but also in certain healing rites and religious beliefs (Aguirre Beltrán 1989). The master's influence is all the greater since there is little to counterbalance it; Mexican students and their teachers know little of the international literature on contemporary black populations. Above all, however, today's descriptions are decontextualized (Martínez Maranto 1994, Cruz 1989), whereas Aguirre Beltrán advocated a political vision of difference that was clearly part of the relations of domination that he so skilfully analysed (Aguirre Beltrán 1972, 1989).

The positive aspect of this line of study is that it has produced updated documentation. Its theoretical limits are soon evident, however, in two slip-ups: first, when it characterizes certain practices as "black," or even "African," and second, when it associates certain practices, or sets of practices, with a collective identity that the researcher arbitrarily calls "black."

In the first case, this characterization of a given practice sends the specialist, namely the ethnologist, back to authenticating a supposedly "African" origin that relegates European or Mesoamerican influences to the background, using a system of exclusion that is apparently oblivious to the particularly intense cultural intermixing that has now been going on for several centuries. The intellectual construction on which these "Afrogenetic" interpretations (Arocha 1999, 204) are based seeks to make up for decades and centuries during which specific "black characteristics" were disregarded, interpreting that disregard as social and institutional racism which must be combated. This outlook derives in large part from the difficulty of thinking about *mestizaje* in any way other than as a negation of the "original" cultures, and its natural corollary is the privileging of "origins" as the exclusive source of legitimacy, to the detriment of a more open, dialectical, and dynamic conceptualization of cultural interactions (Gruzinski 1999). This mental block can obviously be attributed to the way *mestizaje* has been viewed over the years in Mexico, where, from the nineteenth and early twentieth centuries on, theorists saw "the cosmic race" (Vasconcelos 1958: 903-942) as the model of the future, liberated from the cultural atavisms that were considered obstacles to development and national construction. This conception of *mestizaje* having been taken over first by post-revolutionary ideology and then official indigenism, which advocated Indian assimilation and integration (a view now criticized for its Eurocentrism and latent racism), it was never updated as a theory. Instead, it was replaced at the end of the twentieth century by an ethnicizing view of sociopolitical relations that was itself linked both to the recognition of the nation's multicultural and multiethnic character, and to the social and political mobilization of recent decades. Indian groups, in particular, now demand rights and civil participation on the basis of their ethnic identities. The conceptualization of the Afro-Mexican situation is thus based on a model constructed in other spheres.

A major exception to this particularist and exclusionary tendency can be found in southern Veracruz, a region García de León described as "the Afro-Andalucian Caribbean" – a term expressing the inextricable mixture of Caribbean (Cuban in particular, in the late nineteenth and early twentieth centuries) and African influences and the contributions of the European colonists of Spanish extraction.[25] As a number of academic researchers have clearly shown (Alcántara López 2002), music, dance, food, and other cultural manifestations reflect a complex heritage that cannot be appropriated in the name of any particular one of its distant predecessors. Giving a wide berth to the reductive outlines of Afrogenetic interpretation, these researchers highlight the cultural and social creativity of those regional societies – societies that lay claim to distinctly African influences yet definitely do not portray themselves as "black".

The second theoretical blunder involves moving from the individual to the collective, assimilating diverse elements into a constructed, meaningful identity. In southern Veracruz, the Costa Chica, or the warm lands of the Balsas, no one can deny the African origin of various traits, which are joined together with other, clearly Mesoamerican or European features in an arrangement that as a whole is different from that found among the neighbours. Nor does it take any expertise to discern the presence of clearly "black" phenotypes or habitual gestures, whether in dancing or daily life, that distinguish these areas from the Indian and *mestizo* regions of the *altiplano*, for example. Yet until now it has not been proven that this sum of distinctive elements is the basis of a collectively constructed and assumed alterity. Regional identities integrate these elements and many others that, for their part, are not specifically "of African origin:" a shared history, the type of socioeconomic hierarchy, the role of the elites, interregional alliances and rivalries, the environment and the material conditions of production and reproduction—all of these contribute just as much to the construction of a regional "us" as the "cultural characteristics" so often highlighted. Studies on regional identities long ago demonstrated that the cultural field is meaningful only if it is collectively reinterpreted in the broader framework of social, political, and economic relations within the region and with those outside it (Peña 1981, Lomnitz-Adler 1995, Ávila Palafox 1993).

In short, the current ethnographic approach is having trouble discarding the folklorizing and, ultimately, essentialist bias that initially supported it, when it had to "prove" the existence and relevance of "black" or "African traits." By equating identity exclusively with cultural elements, this approach "manufactures" identity on the basis of cultural practices[26] and is likely to foster a simplified, fragmented view of regional societies that are actually much more complex.

Certain recent studies, however, adopt a more modern approach. Taking the debate on national identity and the myths of identity construction as the context for her thinking, Laura Lewis decentralizes the Afro-Mexican issue and dismantles the multiple and often contradictory[27] mechanisms of affiliation and identification, showing the way to a different kind of anthropology. Other researchers in the same region are addressing the same problems in the course of analyzing kinship, production systems, the construction of regional history, or political systems.[28] Without apriorism or ethnic labels, these authors integrate the issues of difference into broader questions about the regional societies and social dynamics,[29] their ideas converging with the orientations already mentioned in respect to historical research in Veracruz, which have proven themselves in other Afro-American regions. It is neither ethnicity nor affiliation with an "ethnic group" that is the organizing factor of social life, but rather practices that integrate identity differences at various levels and in variable configurations depending on the arena and what is at stake (kinship, ritual, production, political interaction, etc.). Very much present in individual and collective daily life, the "black" identity parameter delineates contrasts or proximities, yet without forming a barrier or boundary between groups; consequently, it does not offer much scope for a "multicultural" and "interethnic" conception of society. Yet this is exactly how certain trends now developing in the cultural, social, or political domains are seeking to present it.

The Agents of Ethnicization

Institutions play a decisive role in the ethnological propensity for assigning ethnic traits. The main objective of the "Third Root" programme, which has generated many monographs, is recognizing and disseminating the "specific" and "distinctive" cultural traits of black and *moreno* groups. As though having to make up for centuries of denial in just a few years, researchers now want to prove the existence and richness of a different culture by recording the distinctive aspects of its music, dance, carnival tradition, religion, body movements, or oral tradition – that is, the folkloric fields in which the local traditions are objectively "different" and describable. Thus *jarocha* music in Veracruz is being rediscovered as "black" or even African music, as are the *son de artesa* in the Costa Chica area, the Coyolillo carnival, and even the *zapateado* of Michoacán, a counterpart of the Jalisco version. Cultural events and products (festivals, holidays, conferences, videos, CDs) now proclaim "Africa" on their programmes, and form part of processes of identity invention and reconstruction that are sometimes astonishingly rapid and successful. Thus, for example, the villages of Coyolillo and Yanga in Veracruz are now presented as "black", something almost inconceivable 15 years ago. The hijacking of history by researchers, the establishment of dance and music studios operated by performers, scientific seminars, and visits by foreign black activists and sympathizers are all instruments for this invention of tradition—instruments that are financed by cultural and academic institutions.

Thus, for several years the Mexican cultural institutions have had at their disposal effective tools and channels for disseminating the idea of a black culture, and have quickly interpreted this as the expression of a "black identity." The reaction of the relevant populations to these new conceptions of identity has oscillated from reluctance to support depending on the local context, but in general the subject has elicited neither enthusiasm nor rejection. Their attitude depends rather on the concrete form taken by the cultural action, how well it responds to local expectations (music, for example, is always very successful, as is dance) and whether it may offer advantages of some kind, whether material (access to scholarships, financing) or intangible (contacts with foreigners, regional prestige, activities). The Coyolillo and Yanga carnivals, today portrayed as "black" or even "African," are apparently also the result of a real "identity inoculation," in the words of Sagrario Cruz, the anthropologist who was at one time in charge of these cultural activities at the DGCP.

For the researchers involved, the label "ethnic black" opens doors to the North American black world, which welcomes its "forgotten brothers" of Mexico. Several US anthropologists are writing doctoral theses on the subject of the Mexican black identity (Vaughn 2004), and universities are offering programmes and opportunities for collaboration, whether in Mexico (Xalapa, in March 2004) or the US (for example, the University of Florida, the University of California, and Howard University). In general, these events focus on the struggle against the historic invisibility of blacks in Mexico and the racism implied by that invisibility, and several of them adopt plainly Afrocentric positions (Fauvelle-Aymar, Chrétien, and Perrot 2000), supporting the thesis, for example, that blacks were living in America even before the Spanish conquest. The North American researchers arrive with well-constructed discourses, validated in their home environments by consolidated university institutions, financing, or fellowships. They introduce concepts such as "interethnic relations," "institutional racism," and the "Afro-American diaspora," which are not necessarily those best adapted to the Mexican situation we outlined above. Meetings with Mexican researchers who do not use these theoretical approaches are all the more delicate since they take place against the background of objectively unequal research conditions in the researchers' respective countries of origin. It may be wondered whether these North American academics, often proponents of postcolonial and subaltern theories, are not replicating in Mexico the same mechanisms for imposing theories that they criticize in the US. The same ambiguous relationship, composed of silent or underestimated misapprehensions, characterizes the ties established in the field of Afro-American activism – as witness the strong reaction of a black international leader invited to an annual meeting of México Negro, one of the few organizations that advocates raising the ethnic consciousness of the Afro-Mexican populations. He had trouble finding any common ground with that mixed gathering, and his lecture on the black Latin-American diaspora did not resonate with most of his audience, who were primarily rural inhabitants of the Costa Chica region. He promptly concluded that his audience lacked "black authenticity" and that therefore he did not belong among them.

In contrast to this, however, is the development of other ethnicizing dynamics which are in fact anchored in the daily realities of some of their proponents. For example, the Museo de las Culturas Afromestizas (Museum of Afro-Mestizo Cultures) in Cuajinicuilapa (the Costa Chica area of Guerrero), inaugurated in 1995, is in large part the fruit of an initiative by the local elite, who wanted to create a cultural space that would belong to "the community," without any particular ethnic overtones. In doing so, they joined a nation-wide wave of new community museums and eco-museums created since the end of the 1980s with the encouragement of various institutions, particularly the INAH and the DGCP. Seeking institutional funds and support, these local promoters met with academics and politicians who were themselves interested in Afro issues and could offer already prepared museographic material on the subject. The *afromestizo* orientation of this museum—the only one of its kind in Mexico—was thus constructed through interaction and, largely, chance, but it was smoothly and quite speedily appropriated by a *mestizo* population that saw no special reason not to celebrate this aspect of their cultural patrimony.

Other initiatives arose in the same region, such as AFRICA (Alianza Fortalecimiento de las Regiones Indígenas y Comunidades Afromestizas, or Alliance to Strengthen the Indigenous Regions and Afro-Mestizo Communities), an association created and supported by a group of local teachers and intellectuals interested in regional culture and how it has been influenced by black and Indian populations. The organization briefly mentioned earlier, México Negro, is the brainchild of a black Catholic priest from Trinidad, who moved to Mexico to organize the underprivileged black populations. Even after fifteen years of labour, at every annual meeting he confronted anew the difficulty of rallying crowds around "Afro" issues. Through his social activism and his personal connections, however, he did manage to establish himself as a key agent of institutions in need of organized spokespersons (for production, educational or health programmes, and cultural activities). In these circles he enjoys an unquestionable legitimacy that allows him to publicize the "black" problem far beyond regional boundaries and to attract foreign black militants who in turn disseminate, particularly through the Internet, the idea of an emerging "black consciousness" in Mexico. Working towards that same goal of greater international awareness, México Negro also takes part in certain Afro-American forums (the Afroamerica XXI conferences), although that participation has so far had little notable impact at the local level.

A fourth group of agents, in addition to cultural institutions, academics, and associations, is found in the local political sphere, which is tentatively beginning to integrate the Afro dimension into its activities. For example, during his 2001-2004 term the mayor of Tututepec (Oaxaca) advocated an intercultural approach at the local level through the organization of school exchanges and sports events between the "Indian villages" and the "black communities" (he is one of the few to use this term) that coexist within municipal boundaries. In 2003, for the first time, the municipal recreation committee in Pinotepa

Nacional decided to include an *afromestizo* queen in the Independence Day parade alongside the traditional queens of Spain and Indian America. More recently, the political left on the Oaxaca coast was preparing for the approaching elections (for state governor in July and municipal government in September 2004) by organizing separate meetings specifically directed at *afromestizo* populations (in October 2003) and Indian populations (a few weeks later). These several initiatives have redrawn the public space by legitimizing a differentiated participation by ethnic groups, which now include the *afromestizos* – although, to my knowledge, this applies only to the Costa Chica of Oaxaca.

Conclusion: Avenues of Research

The absence of any external categorization of the *afromestizo* populations by the Mexican state has several consequences. It leaves no potential framework for dialogue and identity confrontation by which an "*afromestizo* group" might be constructed over time, as was the case for the Mames (Chiapas), who, having suffered governmental repression and been forced to abandon their "ancestral customs" in the 1930s and 1940s, are reviving them today through political and ethnic mobilization (Hernández 2001). As a corollary, however, this lack of a framework has provided the freedom to invent other forms of identification.

A primary task would therefore be to pinpoint diverse expressions of identity (political in one area, cultural in another, ethnic in some other region), and to explain their roots at different levels, in various geographical contexts. The immediate purpose of this line of research would be to demonstrate the inconsistence of the ethnicizing positions that contribute today to a stereotyped ethnogenesis of "Afro-Mexicans." The other, more long-term objective would be to understand how space affects the construction of identities through the role it plays in power relations between actors, and between levels of action. It is particularly important to combine the scales of analysis so that instead of juxtaposing monographs, we can identify the modes of interconnection between the different spaces that, as Gupta and Ferguson suggest, shape identities over time. In the case of localized studies, "instead of assuming the autonomy of the primeval community, we need to examine how it was formed as a community out of the interconnected space that always existed" (Gupta and Ferguson 1997, 36). Having shown that the criteria of identification are not the same at the interpersonal level as at the regional or international collective level, we must understand how these different levels mutually influence each other, and, especially, avoid examining each one in isolation.

Taking space into account would allow us to describe and analyze original identity configurations, which the inhabitants interpret and resignify in light of their own interests and current options. In the very heart of the Costa Chica region, for example, models of identification vary from one locality to the next. In one market town where the colonial and later national representatives have imposed a caste system for centuries, "the blacks" see themselves as different from the Indians and the whites. Fifty kilometres away, the historical absence of a ruling white class has allowed the development of a black and *afro-mestizo* microsociety that sees itself as "other" in relation to its Indian neighbours, whereas a black-white opposition does not seem relevant. Slightly farther away still, these various categories are ignored in favour of an idealized image of the "*mestizo*" which integrates differences without resignifying them in ethnic terms. These identity systems are based on very specific economic and political foundations, in which the relations of domination and hierarchy have given meaning to certain "differences" while ignoring others. The white elite of the market town has maintained the differentiated categorization of blacks and Indians in order to perpetuate itself as the economically and politically dominant class, while in the other two cases relations of domination were established within the subordinate groups, or between them and other subordinate groups. In these cases ethnic categorization was much less of a factor.

These contrasting situations might offer the opportunity to revisit the concept of *mestizaje*, avoiding ideologized and globalizing theories in order to focus on local practices. Exploring the multiple facets of identity (collective or personal, assigned or reinvented, national or ethnic, etc.), Wieviorka (2004, 11) states that

> we must not only admit that different issues and problems are at stake here, but, in addition, recognize that in practice they often overlap and combine, never corresponding to sociologically pure types [...]. The debate has nothing to gain by confusing everything, or by borrowing categories relating to one type of problem and applying them to other types. This is why political philosophy, though it might obviously shed some useful light, could never replace concrete knowledge of real, historic situations.

A documented and localized interpretation of *mestizo* experiences might open avenues carrying us far beyond the dead-ends of universalism and particularism. It should be recognized, however, that such an interpretation would have a narrow margin for manoeuvre, with a risk of premature abortion under the influence of North American and international radical movements that endorse ethnicizing categorizations of national societies.

Meanwhile, on the individual level, the affirmation of a "black" alterity is both obvious and painful, because of the constant reminder of difference in social relations that are never free from racism. It also gives rise, as in many other places around the world, to strategies of avoidance or denial that are reflected, for example, in the linguistic field. Designations for the black population vary considerably according to context, and the tendency to euphemism appears to increase with the distance from the place of origin. A person is *"negro"* (black) at home, *"moreno"* (dark-skinned or brunette) in town, and "Mexican" to foreigners. Thus, at the interpersonal level there are spaces of black identification, but also of hybridization and identity interplay that help individuals to position themselves with respect to the other, and to infringe the limits and boundaries between themselves and the other. Conceived thus as a positioning instrument, identification is not stable or fixed, and could help reformulate the global category of *"negro"* or *"afromestizo"* in a more fluid and interactive sense than the current "ethnic" proposals. In this respect, Stuart Hall (1994, 395) speaks of cultural identities being "the points of identification, the unstable points of identification or suture, which are made within the discourses of history and culture. Not an essence but a positioning. Hence, there is always a politics of identity, a politics of position."

In this conception of identity, "cultural traits" are simply tools of social and political positioning that can be manipulated by individuals and groups. By examining the history of these cultural manipulations, we can perhaps understand the evolution of social groups in terms of resistance strategy rather than reproduction, always in the context of interaction with the neighbouring and surrounding societies. Still in the linguistic field, the *afromestizos* of the Costa Chica area have developed a very rich oral tradition, which owes some of its distinctiveness to the linguistic corpus used. As in the Colombian Pacific region, the black populations have retained numerous expressions from "archaic" Spanish. Custodians of a linguistic capital forgotten by others, the *afromestizos* still use it today in their cultural works (poems, ballads) and in daily life, in humorous or ironic expressions that only they understand – expressions that could be thought of as a form of linguistic marronage. They use the master's tool – the language imposed along with slavery – diverting it from its standard usage to make it into an instrument of communication accessible only to some, to insiders. If this avenue is beginning to be explored by linguists (Althoff 1994, Githiora 1999), it will also attract the attention of anthropologists.

Are modern Afro-Mexicans distinguished by a "cultural identity," an "ethnic identity," or a "collective identity"? This article's purpose is to show that this judgement cannot and should not be made, since it implies a simplistic way of thinking that obstructs understanding. Nevertheless, the analytical distinctions remain valid. In fact, Afro-Mexicans activate certain options rather than others, individually or collectively, depending on contexts, spaces, and local relations of subordination. The processes of constructing identity are for the moment still unequal in social and geographic space, largely because of or thanks to the fact that the state and institutions have no interest in a marginal minority group without any strategic resources. Efforts to create a black Mexican "ethnic group" that could join with its "diaspora brothers" are emerging most clearly outside of the regional societies and the country itself. These tendencies, if confirmed, would run the risk of erasing far more complex processes, which do not seek to set up any clear or definitive separation between the desire for a distinct identity and the historic reality of *mestizaje*, but rather combine the two.

Notes

1.   Translated by Martha Grenzeback. Adaptation of: Odile, Hoffmann. Negros y afromestizos en México: viejas y nuevas lecturas de un mundo olvidado. *Revista Mexicana de Sociología* 68(1): 103-135.

2.   Like other social categories (workers, women, the poor), ethnic categories are constructions with changing boundaries that analysis cannot reduce to stable, easily definable groups according to "objective" criteria, as is the case for legally constituted nationalities. In contrast to actual nationalities, both ethnonyms (Mixtecs, Mames) and ethnic categories (Indians, Afro-Mestizos) describe social groups that are constantly redefining themselves, rather than legal or social categories with clearly established limits.

3.   See Agudelo1999, 151-176.

4.   The "indigenous" population is estimated at 10.5-12.5 percent of the total population of the country, depending on the criteria used and how they are combined: use of an Indian language, or member of a household in which the head or the head's spouse speaks an Indian language. See Serrano Carreto, Embriz Osorio and Fernández Ham 2002).

5.   I have adopted the term Afro-Mexican because it is becoming common in Mexico, just as similar usages have spread in other countries of Latin America (Afro-Colombian, Afro-Brazilian, etc.) The word "Afrodescendants is rarely used and is more specific to international debates. However, there is no consensus on the use of "black", neither among researchers nor among the populations in question, which often do not recognize themselves as such and use their regional names instead.

6.   This is true even of the "multicultural" version of the nation instituted by the constitutional reform of 1992, which amended

Article 4 to state that the Mexican nation has a multicultural composition originating in its indigenous "peoples".

7. This racism is of course not confined to the realm of interpersonal interactions, and affects society as a whole, as much today as in the past—for example, during the Mexican Revolution which recast the national identity without managing to "fix" the problem of racism. See Knight 1990.

8. The Yanga rebellion in the early seventeenth century and especially the revolt of 1735 in the Córdoba region (Veracruz) led to the formation of *palenques*, villages of free blacks. The first was founded in 1640 under the name of San Lorenzo de los Negros (today called Yanga), followed, one century later, by the village of Nuestra Señora de Amapa. See Naveda Chávez-Hita 1987.

9. At the time of the 1777 census, a priest reported the difficulties involved in determining people's "caste", noting that in his parish "there is no separate census for Spaniards alone, another for the mestizos, another for mulattos, and another for the Indians because all the castes live in the town and in one house it is common to meet people of every category; even in a single family the husband may be of one status, the wife another, and the children yet another". Quoted by Sánchez Santiró 2003, 41.

10. That is, well before emancipation in France (finally achieved in 1848), Colombia (1851), the United States (1865), Cuba (1886), and Brazil (1888).

11. Certain clichés, though persistent, do not correspond to the historical evidence. One of them is the idea that the black population is confined to certain regions, namely the Atlantic (Veracruz-Tabasco) and Pacific coasts (the Costa Chica area of Guerrero and Oaxaca). As mentioned previously, blacks were initially to be found throughout the national territory, and certain regions traditionally characterized as "white" or "creole", such as Jalisco or the northern part of the country, had very substantial black populations in the seventeenth century, now gone or effectively "diluted" by racial mixing. See Becerra 2002, Nájera 2002.

12. Thus, we are dealing here with customary categories, as will be seen further on. See Pépin Lehalleur 2003, Campos 1999, Neff 1986.

13. "It cannot be denied that in hybridization the black factor was predominant and that consequently mestizos in Cuajinicui-

lapa today are primarily black—that is, afromestizos" (Aguirre Beltrán 1989, 65).

14. In the introduction to his ethnographic work, Aguirre Beltrán reaffirmed the exceptional nature of the Costa Chica situation, reminding readers that "blacks no longer exist as a distinct group." (Aguirre Beltrán 1989, 7). Aguirre Beltrán does not capitalize categories denoting identity (indians, blacks, mixtecs), adhering to the normal usage in Mexico.

15. In particular, the foundation of the Instituto Nacional Indigenista (INI—National Indigenist Institute) in 1948.

16. See Aguirre Beltrán's prologue to the 1972 edition of his work *La población negra en Mexico*.

17. Notably in the states of Guanajuato and Veracruz.

18. Centre of Studies on Asia and Africa, Colegio de México.

19. Caribbean research group.

20. Alberro 1988, Castañón González 2002.

21. Martínez Montiel 1993a, 1993b. All these references are merely token examples, since there are too many studies to cite them all here; see the bibliographies cited further on.

22. See Martínez Montiel, "La cultura africana: tercera raíz".

23. See Recondo 2001.

24. Flanet 1977. Aguirre Beltrán often mentions "the violent ethos" of the blacks of the Costa Chica; see Aguirre Beltrán 1989.

25. García de Leon 1992, 1993. The Indians had been swiftly decimated in these regions following the Spanish conquest, surviving only in the mountain enclaves of Santa Marta and the foothills around Playa Vicente.

26. Compare with Agier's "identity cultures" (Agier 2001).

27. In the case of the Costa Chica area of Oaxaca. See Lewis 2000.

28. On kinship, see Díaz Pérez 2003, 247. On production systems, see Quiroz Malca 1998. On the construction of regional history, see Pépin Lehalleur 2000. On political systems, see Lara Millán 2003.

29. As Levine remarks, the problem of categorization is not posited a priori but when we see "how ethnic categories become salient components of social and cultural action" (Levine 1999, 168).

30. For Colombia, see Losonczy 2002.

31. At both the federal and state levels: Dirección General de Culturas Populares, Instituto Veracruzano de Cultura, Instituto Oaxaqueño de Cultura, Consejo Nacional para la Cultura y las Artes.

32. It is impossible to list here all the festivals or cultural events of this kind, but we will mention the annual Afro-Caribbean festival of Veracruz, created at the end of the 1980s; the seminar "Africa in Mexico" held in 2004 in Xalapa, and the various manifestations of "black music and dance" in Mexico and the provinces. Common to all is the effort to reinstate the Afro-Mexican culture by emphasizing its African "roots".

33. On Coyolillo, see Martínez Maranto 1994; on Yanga, see Cruz Carretero et al. 1990.

34. This theory is based almost exclusively on the negroid features of the Olmec heads in Veracruz. At the "Africa in Mexico" conference held in Xalapa in March 2004, a number of nationally respected archaeologists supported this theory. See de Brizuela 2004, Cuevas Fernández 2004.

35. Interviews held in Cuajinicuilapa, January 2003.

36. At the end of the nineteenth century, an observer remarked that the inhabitants of Cuajinicuilapa "are of African race" and that for that reason they "speak ancient Spanish". Quoted by Aguirre Beltrán 1989, 63.

Bibliography

Agier, Michel. 2001. Le temps des cultures identitaires. Enquête sur le retour du diable à Tumaco (Pacifique colombien). *L'Homme* 157: 87-114.

Agudelo, Carlos Efren. 1999. Participation politique des populations noires en Colombie. *Cahier des Amériques Latines* 30: 151-176.

Aguirre Beltrán, Gonzalo. 1972 [1946]. *La población negra de México: estudio etnohistórico.* Mexico City: Fondo de Cultura Económica.

Aguirre Beltrán, Gonzálo. 1989 [1958].*Cuijla: esbozo etnográfico de un pueblo negro.* Mexico City: Fondo de Cultura Económica.

Alberro, Solange B. de. 1988. Negros y Mulatos: la integración dolorosa. In *Inquisición y sociedad en México, 1571-1700.* Mexico City: FCE.

Alcántara López, Álvaro. 2002. "Negros y afromestizos del puerto de Veracruz. Impresiones de lo popular durante los siglos XVII y XVIII". In *La Habana/Veracruz, Veracruz/La Habana, Las dos orillas*, coord. Bernardo García Díaz and Sergio Guerra Vilaboy. Veracruz: Universidad Veracruzana: 166-175.

Althoff, Daniel. 1994. Afro Mestizo Speech from Costa Chica, Guerrero: From Cuaji to Cuijla. *Language Problems and Language Planning* 18: 242-256.

Argyriadis, Kali and Capone, Stefania. 2004. Cubanía et santería. Les enjeux politiques de la transnationalisation religieuse (La Havane—Miami). *Civilisations* 51: 81-137.

Arocha, Jaime. 1999. *Ombligados de Ananse. Hilos ancestrales y modernos en el pacífico colombiano*. Bogotá: Universidad Nacional de Colombia-CES.

Ávila Palafox, Ricardo. 1993. "Elites, región e identidad en el occidente de México". In *Identidades, nacionalismos y regiones*, comp. Ricardo Avila Palafox and Tomás Calvo Buezas. Guadalajara: Universidad de Guadalajara/Universidad Complutense de Madrid.

Barabas, Alicia and Bartolomé, Miguel. 1986. *Etnicidad y pluralismo cultural: la dinámica étnica en Oaxaca*. Mexico City: Colección Regiones-CNCA.

Barth, Fredrik. 1981. "Ethnic Groups and Boundaries". In *Process and Form in Social Life: The Selected Essays of Fredrik Barth*, ed. Adam Kuper. London: Routledge & Kegan Paul: 198-227.

Barth, Fredrik. 1994. "Enduring and Emerging Issues in the Analysis of Ethnicity. In *The Anthropology of Ethnicity: Beyond "Ethnic Groups and Boundaries"*, ed. Hans Vermeulen and Cora Govers. Amsterdam: Het Spinhuis: 11-32.

Becerra, Celina. 2002. Población Africana en una sociedad ranchera. *Estudios Jalisciences* 49: 7-19.

de Brizuela, Gladys Casimir. 2004. "Hubo negros en América Precolombina. En busca de una metodología". *3rd Annual Conference Africa en México*. Xalapa, Veracruz, 22-24 March 2004.

Campos, Luis Eugenio. 1999. "Negros y morenos. La población afromexicana de la Costa Chica de Oaxaca". In *Configuraciones étnicas en Oaxaca. Perspectivas etnográficas para las autonomías*, coord. Alicia M. Barabas and Miguel A. Bartolomé. Vol. II. Mexico City: CNCA/INAH-INI: 145-182;

Carroll, Patrick J. 1991. *Blacks in Colonial Veracruz, Race, Ethnicity and Regional Development.* Austin: University of Texas Press.

Castañón González, Guadalupe. 2002. *Punición y rebeldía de los negros en la nueva España en los siglos XVI y XVII.* Xalapa: Instituto Veracruzano de la Cultura, Colección Sextante.

Castillo Gómez, Amaranta Arcadia. 2000. "El papel de los estereotipos en las relaciones interétnicas: mixtecos, mestizos y afromestizos en Pinotepa Nacional, Oaxaca, México". Unpublished thesis. México: Escuela Nacional de Antropología e Historia.

Cervantes Delgado, Roberto. 1984. "La Costa Chica. Indios, negros y mestizos". In *Estratificación étnica y relaciones interétnicas,* coord. Margarita Nolasco. Mexico City: INAH, Colección Científica #135: 37-50.

Chávez Carvajal, María Guadalupe. 1995. "Negros y mulatos en Michoacán". In *Tradición e identidad.* Coord. Agustín Jacinto Zavala and Alvaro Ochoa Serrano. Zamora: El Colegio de Michoacán: 396-397.

Cruz, Sagrario. 1989. "Identidad en una comunidad afromestiza del centro de Veracruz: la población de Mata Clara". Unpublished thesis. Pueblo: Fundación Universidad de las Américas.

Cruz Carretero, Sagrario et al. 1990. *El Carnaval en Yanga: notas y comentarios sobre una fiesta de la negritud.* Mexico City: Consejo Nacional para la Cultura y las Artes.

Cuevas Fernández, Hector. 2004. "¿Presencia Negra en el México arqueológico?". *3rd Annual Conference "Africa en México".* Xalapa, Veracruz, 22-24 March 2004.

Cunin, Elisabeth. 2002. *Métissage et multiculturalisme en Colombie. Le "noir" entre apparences et appartenances.* Paris: L"Harmattan-IRD, Collection Connaissances des Hommes.

Delgado Calderón, Alfredo. 2000. "La conformación de regiones en el Sotavento veracruzano: una aproximación histórica". In *El Sotavento veracruzano. Procesos sociales y dinámicas territoriales.* Coord. Eric Léonard and Emilia Velásquez. Mexico City: CIESAS-IRD.

Díaz Pérez, María Cristina. 1994. "Descripción etnográfica de las relaciones de parentesco en tres comunidades afromestizas de la Costa Chica de Guerrero". Unpublished thesis, Mexico City: Escuela Nacional de Antropología e Historia.

Díaz Pérez, María Cristina. 2003. *Queridato, matrifocalidad y crianza en tres comunidades de la Costa Chica*. Mexico City: CNCA/ Unidad Regional Guerrero-PACMYC.

Fauvelle-Aymar, Xavier, Chrétien, J. P and Perrot, C. H. 2000. *Afrocentrismes. L'histoire des Africains entre Egypte et Amérique*. Paris: Karthala, 2000.

Flanet, Véronique. 1977. *Viviré si Dios quiere. Un estudio de la violencia en la mixteca de la costa*. Serié de Antropología Social #55. Mexico City: INI.

García de Leon, Antonio. 1992. El Caribe afroandaluz: permanencias de una civilización popular. *La Jornada semanal* (Mexico City), 12 Jan. 1992: 27-33;

García de Leon, Antonio. 1993. "Comunidad histórica e identidad regional: los casos de Chiapas y Veracruz". In *Identidades, nacionalismos y regiones*, comp. Ricardo Avila Palafox and Tomás Calvo Buezas. Guadalajara: Universidad de Guadalajara/Universidad Complutense de Madrid: 187-197.

Githiora, Chege John. 1999. "Lexical Variation in Discourse: Socioracial Terms and Identity in an Afromexican Community". Unpublished doctoral thesis, Michigan State University.

Glazer, Nathan and Moynihan, Daniel. 1975. *Ethnicity: Theory and Experience.*Cambridge: Harvard University Press;

Gruzinski, Serge. 1999. *La pensée métisse*. Paris: Fayard.

Guevera Sanginés, María. 1994. "Participación de los africanos en el desarrollo del Guanajuato colonial". In *Presencia Africana en México*. Eds. Luz María Martínez Montiel. Mexico City: Consejo Nacional para la Cultura y las Artes, Colección claves de América Latina, serie Nuestra Tercera Raíz:133-198;

Gupta,j Akhil and Ferguson, James. 1997. "Beyond "Culture": Space, Identity, and the Politics of Difference". In *Culture, Power, Place Explorations in Critical Anthropology*, eds. Akhil Gupta and James Ferguson. Durham, NC, and London: Duke University Press: 33-51.

Gutiérrez Avila, Miguel Angel. 1988. *Corrido y violencia: entre los afromestizos de la Costa Chica de Guerrero y Oaxaca*. Chilpancingo: Universidad Autónoma de Guerrero.

Hall, Stuart. 1994. "Cultural Identity and Diaspora". In *Colonial Discourse and Post-Colonial Theory: A Reader*. Ed. Patrick Williams and Laura Chrisman. New York: Columbia University Press: 392-403.

Hernández, Aida. 2001. *La otra frontera. Identidades múltiples en el Chiapas poscolonial.* Mexico City: CIESAS—Miguel Angel Porrúa.

Herrera Casasús, María Luisa 1994. "Raices africanas en la población de Tamaulipas". In *Presencia Africana en México*. Eds. Luz María Martínez Montiel. Mexico City: Consejo Nacional para la Cultura y las Artes, Colección claves de América Latina, serie Nuestra Tercera Raíz: 463-523.

Hoffmann, Odile. 2001. "Flux et reflux des catégories identitaires. Une lecture des politiques foncières au Mexique et en Colombie". In *Les territoires de l'Etat-Nation en Amérique Latine.* Coord. M.F. Prévot Schapira and H. Rivière d'Arc. Paris: IHEAL Editions: 101-120.

Knight, Alan. 1990. "Racism, Revolution and Indigenismo: Mexico, 1910-1940". In *The Idea of Race in Latin America, 1870-1940.* Ed. Richard Graham. Austin: University of Texas Press: 71-112.

Lara Millán, Gloria. 2003. "Raíces de color. Afromexicanos en la construcción ciudadana, Costa Chica, Oaxaca". Unpublished master's thesis. Mexico City: Universidad Autónoma Metropolitana.

Levine, Hal B. 1999. Reconstructing ethnicity. *Journal of the Royal Anthropological Institute* 5: 165-180.

Lewis, Laura. 2000. Blacks, Black Indians, Afromexicans: The Dynamics of Race, Nation and Identity in a Mexican *Moreno* Community (Guerrero). *American Ethnologist* 27: 898-926.

Lomnitz-Adler, Claudio. 1995. *Las salidas del laberinto. Cultura e ideología en el espacio nacional mexicano.* Mexico City: Joaquín Mortín-Planeta.

Losonczy, Anne Marie. 2002. "De cimarrones a colonos y contrabandistas: figuras de movilidad transfronteriza en la zona dibullera del Caribe colombiano" In *Afrodescendientes en las Américas. Trayectorias sociales e identitarias.* Eds. C. Mosquera, M. Pardo and O. Hoffmann. Bogotá: Universidad Nacional, ICANH, IRD, ILSA: 215-244.

Martínez Maranto, Alfredo. 1994. "Dios pinta como quiere: Identidad y cultura en un pueblo afromestizo de Veracruz". In *Presencia Africana en México*. Eds. Luz María Martínez Montiel. Mexico

City: Consejo Nacional para la Cultura y las Artes, Colección claves de América Latina, serie Nuestra Tercera Raíz: 525-573.

Moedano Navarro, Gabriel. 1992. "Bibliohemerografía histórica y etnohistórica sobre la población de origen africano en México". In *Aportaciones a la investigación de archivos del México colonial y a la bibliohemerografía afromexicanista*. Ed. Emma Pérez-Rocha and Gabriel Moedano Navarro. Mexico City: INAH, Colección Fuentes, Serie Bibliografías: 37-64;

Moedano Navarro, Gabriel. 1997. "Los afromestizos y su contribución a la identidad cultural en el pacífico sur: el caso de la tradición oral en la Costa Chica". In *Pacífico Sur: ¿Una región cultural?*. México City: CNCA: 1-7.

Martínez Montiel, Luz María. 1993a. "La pluralidad del mestizaje". In *III Encuentro Nacional de Afromexicanistas, Colima*. Ed. Luz María Martínez and Juan Carlos Reyes. Colima: CNCA-Gobierno del Estado de Colima: 20-40.

Martínez Montiel, Luz María. 1993b. "La cultura africana: tercera raíz". In *Simbiosis de culturas. Los inmigrantes y su cultura en México*. Comp. Guillermo Bonfil Batalla. Mexico City: FCE: 111-180.

Martínez Montiel, Luz María. 1994. *Presencia Africana en México*. Mexico City: Consejo Nacional para la Cultura y las Artes, Colección claves de América Latina, serie Nuestra Tercera Raíz.

Nájera, Mario Alberto. 2002. Los afrojaliscienses. *Estudios Jaliscienses* 49: 20-32.

Naveda Chávez-Hita, Adriana. 1987. *Esclavos negros en las haciendas azucareras de Córdoba, Veracruz, 1690-1830*. Xalapa, Veracruz: Universidad Veracruzana, Historias Veracruzanas.

Neff, Francoise. 1986. "Reflexiones sobre la identidad del afromestizo de la Costa Chica de Guerrero". In *Palabras devueltas*. Ed. Jesús Jáuregui and Yves-Marie Gourio. Mexico City: INAH-IFAL-CEMCA: 71-74.

Palmer Colin, Alphonsus. 1993. "Afro-Mexican Culture and Consciousness during the Sixteenth and Seventeenth Centuries". In *Global Dimensions of the African Diaspora*. Ed. Joseph E. Harris. Washington DC: Howard University Press: 125-135.

Peña, Guillermo de la. 1981. Los estudios regionales y la antropología social en México. *Relaciones. Estudios de Historia y Sociedad* 1(8): 43-93.

Pépin Lehalleur, Marielle. 2000. "¿Existe el regionalismo popular? Reflexiones a partir de una región pluri-étnica". In *El Sotavento veracruzano. Procesos sociales y dinámicas territoriales.* Coord. Eric Léonard and Emilia Velásquez. Mexico City: CIESAS-IRD.

Pépin Lehalleur, Marielle. 2003. "¿Existe el regionalismo popular? Reflexiones a partir de una región pluri-étnica". In *Territorios, Actores y Poder, regionalismos emergentes en México.* Coord. J. Preciado Coronado et al. Guadalajara and Merida: Universidad de Guadalajara-Universidad Autónoma de Yucatán: 25-48.

Quiroz Malca, Haydee. 1998. "Las mujeres y los hombres de la sal. Un proceso de producción y reproducción cultural en la Costa Chica de Guerrero". Unpublished doctoral thesis. Mexico City: Universidad Iberoamericana.

Recondo, David. 2001. Mexique: multiculturalisme et démocratisation dans le Oaxaca. *Problèmes d'Amérique latine* 41: 45-70.

Sánchez Santiró, Ernest. 2003. *Padrón del arzobispado de México 1777.* Mexico City: AGN.

Serrano Carreto, Enrique, Embriz Osorio, Arnulfo and Fernández Ham, Patricia. coords. 2002. *Indicadores socioeconómicos de los pueblos indígenas de México.* Mexico City: INI-PNUD México-CONAPO.

Touraine, Alain. 1988. Modernité et spécificités culturelles. *Revue Internationale des Sciences Sociales* XV: 497-511.

Vasconcelos, José. 1958. "La raza cósmica". In *Obras Completas,* Vol. II. Mexico City: Libreros Mexicanos: 903-942.

Vaughn, Bobby. 2004. "Negros, una apreciación global breve". Available online at www.mexconnect.com/mx_/feature/ethnic/bv/costa.htm

Velasco, Baltazar. 2002. La costa chica. *Revista Fandango* 2: 1-2

Velázquez Gutiérrez, María Elisa. 1994. "Mujeres afromexicanas en la Nueva España". Paper presented at the IV Encuentro de Afromexicanistas. Veracruz: Instituto Veracruzano de Cultura.

Wachtel, Nathan. 1992. Note sur le problème des identités collectives dans les Andes méridionales. *L'Homme* 122-124(32) (2-3-4): 39-52.

Wieviorka, Michel. 2004. "Identités culturelles et démocratie". Paris : Séminaire ERSIPAL-IHEAL, June.

Chapter 5

An Ethno-Political Trend on the Costa Chica, Mexico (1980-2000)[1]

Gloria Lara

Introduction

In this paper, I want to analyze the emergence of the ethno-political referent in Mexico, more precisely on the Costa Chica of Oaxaca and Guerrero. Using data obtained during a long and intense period of field research,[2] I describe how a "black trend" has been structuring itself from the years 1990-2000 onwards; I reconstruct its genealogy and its internal diversity. This will permit me to avoid two pitfalls, one which tends to underrate black mobilization in Mexico, alleging its "lack of authenticity," its recent character, and its weak local acceptance and the other, to the contrary, overrates the role and impact of Afro-descendent organizations, which only group together a few dozen individuals – even fewer in some cases. Whatever the importance and dynamism of this trend may be, its existence can no longer be denied and deserves analytical attention. This is what I aim to do in this text but first I will set out the context of the debate in which this ethno-political construction is situated.

"The other", between ethnic and racial

There are differences that surround hierarchical systems amongst the different populations inhabiting Latin America. The ethnic referents are often related to ancestral origin, territory, culture, traditional practices, clothing, language, forms of organization, systems of authority and self-government amongst others that constitute identifiers of a people, ethnic group or nation. In this "classical" conception of ethnic identity (Bartolomé 1997, Giménez, 2000), the emphasis on one or various of these referents depends on the formation of the State and on the historical transformations on which the conception and the imaginary of otherness are based.

It is the indigenous population that has been identified almost exclusively in the collective imagination as a form of cultural otherness. The Afro-descendent populations are barely recognized in these terms and even in other countries are "unthinkable in the dominant imaginaries of ethnic difference" (Restrepo 2007, 480), while "black" distinguishes more in racial terms.

In the context of multi-cultural policies, at the beginning of the 1990s in some countries like Colombia, Nicaragua, Ecuador, Honduras, and Guatemala, the Afro-descendent populations underwent a process of ethnicization that resulted in the recognition of their own culture, with associated collective rights. In this process, we can observe certain "models of ethnicity" put into practice by each country that reflect the place that the Afro-descendent populations occupy in the nation's image of itself.

Restrepo (2007, 480) identifies three cases of ethnicity model:

1. When "the black populations are equivalent to the indigenous ones in the place they occupy in the contemporary "structures of otherness,"
2. When "Afro-descendants are circumstantially equivalent to the indigenous populations in these structures," and
3. When "the Afro-descendant populations are practically unthinkable for these equivalencies."

The author maintains that the first model is the least common in Latin America, while the third is the most generalized. These can be seen in the cases of Colombia and Peru. In Colombia a paradigm of black ethnicity was constructed in which "black cultures" are referred to – within models of indigenous ethnicity (Agudelo 2005) – that is to say, populations with their own culture, bearers of traditional production practices, relationship with nature, forms of social organization, and territorial appropriation, but circumscribed to the regional space of Colombia's Pacific coast. (Ng'weno 2007) In the second case, the Afro-Peruvians are not considered to be a people, so they are recognized as bearers of ethnicity in the same way as the indigenous Andeans who constitute the paradigm of indigenous culture (Greene 2007).

In the case of Mexico the idea of "the other" is also embodied principally in "the indigenous" population. Up until now, the Afro-descendent population has not been represented in the "national" collective imagination.[3] This is characterized by a great degree of heterogeneity, both due to factors of geographical location (urban and rural, in small localities as well as the metropolis, in all regions of the country) and to forms of insertion in society and the relations that this population maintain with other social groups. The use of the concept of the mestizo is an ideological component in the construction of the nation since the early twentieth century and the resulting myth about the "mix of races" which incorporated indigenous people but not the Afro-descendent population. Even this first studies of "black populations" carried out in the middle of the century (Aguirre 1946) considered that this population would disappear and integrate itself with the mestizo. Tendentiously the myth of the mestizo was reaffirmed at the same time as the question of "the black" was concluded and the issue of slavery as a subject for debate was avoided (see the research project *Afrodesc*, 2008, *www.ird.fr/afrodesc*). The issue of discrimination and the participation of the Afro-descendent population was silenced in national history and relegated to peripheral spaces and roles.

The Afro-descendent population in Mexico is almost always identified by phenotypic features. The history and power relations that frame the collective imagination show us different elaborations of "black" based on mestizo hierarchies and different patterns of racial categorization. For example, in Veracruz, the black presence forges, along with that of the indigenous and Spanish presence, the "jarocho" identity that does not form part of the set of ethnic groups but instead appears as a regional identification (southern Veracruz) that is assumed to be mestizo (Hoffmann 2007b). The cultural features inherited from Africa are materialized in the gastronomy and artistic expressions of "the jarochos" that can be seen in celebrations as part of the regional folklore. Other referents that demonstrate and construct the idea of "black" are related to the close ties with the population of the Caribbean through the circulation of people, ideas, practices and merchandise. The particular characteristics of what is considered "afro" shows a "culture that is shared" through music, dance and the fiesta, that tend to be associated with sexuality (body and behavior) and festivities.

In contrast, on the Costa Chica of Guerrero and Oaxaca, the contents of "black" are not only different but also in some cases present contrast within the region itself. Indeed, it is a pluriethnic region inhabited by an indigenous population (Amuzgo, Chatino, Mixteco, Nahua, and Tlapaneco) and mestizo (where we find the "whites," the "rich," and the "people of reason."[4] In this regional space the construction of "black" can be seen to be based on the naturalization of spaces according to a "racialized spatial model" that associates the mountainous zone with the indigenous population, the municipal capitals and urban centers with mestizos, and the plains and some villages with the "darks." At the same time, it is assumed that the social and economic hierarchies are articulated with ethnic differences (Hoffmann 2007b). The "cultural features" can be seen mainly in dance and music. The political expressions of these populations are different in each state. For example, the government of Oaxaca has a discourse with broad criteria for recognizing and vindicating cultural difference. In some cases, it has even taken initiatives that go beyond collective pressure and demands.

On the other hand, in the government of the state of Guerrero, caution can be observed on some topics, despite discourses adorned with multiculturalism. Today, old stereotypes inherited from the colonial period survive and are reproduced that represent black people as violent, lazy, fierce, resistant individuals, etc. (Lara 2007). These phenotypic differences are associated with "cultural characteristics" and are activated in different day-to-day circumstances, but most evidently when people with Afro features find themselves outside their local context and face to face with external agents, especially from public institutions. These representations of "black" became legitimized over time as well as in texts or actions carried out by different government institutions and sometimes by academics who study this population.[5]

The construction of ethno-political discourse on the Costa-Chica

In the 1990s, important socio-political transformations became evident that were a referent for the struggles for the recognition of citizens and cultural rights in Mexico. Some were oriented towards the decentralization in the country and others towards the recognition of difference. Amongst these changes are the recognition of cultural diversity in the Mexican Constitution; the declaration of a multicultural and pluri-ethnic nation of 1992, the uprising of the Zapatista Army of National Liberation in 1994, the diversification of social actors and organizations in the public sphere, and the strengthening of local and regional government (municipal reform). These events were associated with the application of policies aimed at the reduction of the state and public decentralization that widened the social gap in terms of inequality. In this context, a number of collectives regrouped themselves around other identities that permitted them to open up spaces for participation in order to defend their own projects and alternatives for development and global insertion.

On the other hand, the Mexican state incorporated into its discourses some of the policies of international agencies that conditioned funding to the incorporation of the ethno-racial variation in development projects. Here I am referring to the Inter-American Development Bank (IAD), the World Bank (IBRD), the United Nations Development Programme, and UNESCO, which formed part of the drive towards the policies of recognition. In agreement with multicultural discourse, the international organization, foundations and NGOs for cooperation and development also included actions in the agendas aimed at cultural recognition, development and capacity building amongst ethnic actors, in order for them to participate and influence political processes on different levels.[6]

In this context, different actors on the Costa Chica that affirmed themselves to be black, Afro-Mexican or Afro-mestizo have carried out actions to support their own ethnic recognition, specific rights and public policies favorable to the development of their communities. The Afro-descendent populations that we are talking about live mainly in the localities near the Pacific coast in the states of Guerrero and Oaxaca, although they also reside in communities where the mestizo and indigenous population make up the majority. It is a pluriethnic region (Pepin-Lehalleur 2003) where there is an intense interaction between groups and individuals of different ethnic adscription, closely linked to the integration of economic activities in the zone.

The emergence of the Afro-descendent ethnic question that can be observed on the Costa Chica can be explained by the internal dynamics of the individuals and collectives promoting it (internal organization, willingness to participate, group strengthening, expansion) as well as the surrounding conditions in which it is developing and the influence of the national level political processes mentioned above. We can identify two moments in the emergence of the Afro issue: 1) the recuperation of African contributions, the "third root", to regional cultural heritage, in the form of regional dances and music since the middle of the 1980s.; and 2) the politicization of discourse and public expression in favor of Afro recognition in different regional, state, national, and international forums during the first few years of the twenty-first century.[7]

In the first moment, both in Oaxaca and Guerrero, the topic of the Afro-descendent population first appeared in government agencies. The "Third Root" program that emerged during the 1980s was the starting point for actions related to research on the cultural substratum of the Afro-descendent population in national culture. This program organized a number of seminars, encounters, and research that enriched ways of understanding slavery as a system (Naveda 1999). During the same decade, a number of researchers from the INAH and Culturas Populares decided to retrieve the Afro-mestizo tradition on the Cost Chica. The first fruits of this institutional intervention were the collections of corridos, verses, and sones (some produced as discs) as well as the presentation of Afro-mestizo dances outside the region. The Casa de Cultura in the community of San Nicolás Tolentino was also created and the Museo de Culturas Afromestizas de Cuajinicuilapa, in the state of Guerrero. The creation of this museum merits special attention due to the intervention of the three levels of government (federal, state and municipal) in its the construction, and the participation of citizens' groups in the community (a number of them professionals and tradespeople). The good will of public officials was an important factor in getting the project off the ground and the local people who contributed to the museum still operate it today.

At the local level, the motives of local leaders, collectives, and some professionals for approaching the issue of "black" culture varied.[8] The leaders identified with the issue because most of them had a profession or held a position of authority in their community. These conditions provided them with a certain capacity for movement, access to information, contacts outside the community, and the opportunity to acquire social prestige within their communities. By the 1990s, the organizations dedicated to cultural promotion and recognition of the "third root" were the Museo Comunitario de Cuajinicuilapa in Guerrero, México Negro A.C., and the Casa del Pueblo de José María Morelos (later some of its members formed the organization Africa, A.C. on the coast of Oaxaca).

At that time, the cultural contents were centered to a great extent on the search for and re-affirmation of specific cultural features expressed in the dances, music, and characteristic forms of speaking Spanish. These, along with physical appearance, were interpreted as markers of regional "black or Afromestizo culture," given the absence of other categories that are often used in relation to the indigenous population (clothing, language, historical cultural heritage, and memory). Later, the same features would constitute the fabric on which make incursions into politics and vindicate, more insistently, the legal recognition of the Afro-descendent. At that time, the core of cultural content was aimed at finding "African roots" that in same way would give order to the difference despite the risk of diluting the complex relations in various aspects of regional society as well as the ways in which the Afro-descendent populations inserted themselves in it.

However, in the initial construction of what is "black" amongst the leaders and collectives, it was possible to discern different visions that, on the one hand, reveal differentiated social processes in local societies,[9] and on the other denote unequal social capital, on the basis of which the actors reformulated ideas and concepts about this question. Let us look at this in more detail.

For both the collectives on Costa Chica in Guerrero and in Oaxaca, one objective was the recognition of the "Afro-Mexican third root." However, there were (and still are) nuances in their conceptions that distanced them and, to a certain extent, have had an influence on the alliances between groups. For example, in Cuajinicuilapa, Guerrero, the vindication of the third root in national history, its cultural contribution, and national construction are shared. Cultural recognition is understood to be linked with the indigenous and mestizo populations without this meaning the negation of the third root or its particular cultural features. Local intellectuals put forward interpretations that understand it has a regional popular culture.[10] There is even talk of a "coastal culture," understood as a regional identity in which the Afro root is immersed. In this case, skin color is not the characteristic that is most emphasized, although nor is it denied that appearance is an element of identity, "because there are many mixtures and tones."

On the coast of Oaxaca, the elaboration of what is "black" vindicates recognition in history and national construction, but in contrast to what we have seen, for the neighbors from Guerrero "Cultural features" are understood as particular elements of an "ethnic group." In this case, although proximity with the indigenous and mestizo population is not denied, a vision of separate racial groups is denoted, confining each one to certain spaces and with phenotypic features that make their presence evident and there is more insistence on the vindication of "blacks" or" black peoples" where skin color is emphasized as a particular ethnic feature. However, not everyone identifies themselves with this racial category and some even try to distance themselves from it due to daily experiences of discrimination and racism that they have suffered and suffer in the region and outside it.

These representations are mediated by the discourses of the respective state formations in Oaxaca and Guerrero. Particularly in Oaxaca, the multicultural model is guided by an ethnic approach that aims at territorializing identities, focusing on material culture and naturalizing racial and cultural limits. The political discourse of state governments from the middle of the 1980s until today vindicates ethnic diversity and proclaims the defense of indigenous rights. In Oaxaca a number of constitutional reforms were carried through in which the multicultural composition of the state is recognized (1990); for the election of local authorities the customary system is recognized (1995) and the Law on the Rights of Indigenous Peoples and Communities of the State of Oaxaca was passed (1998) recognizing the existence of Afro-Mexicans as an "ethnic group".

In addition, the referents that to some extent contributed to and balanced discursive contents on ethnicity came to the fore thanks to research done by anthropologists and other specialists. For example, texts by Gutiérrez Avila and Moedano (Cited in Motta 2006), that have emphasized oral manifestations on the Costa Chica as clearly having African roots. Others filtered through during the intervention of Mexican and foreign visitors at the encounters of "black peoples" convened by the organization Mexico Negro A.C. José Motta (2006) describes the intervention of an official from the United States in a meeting of black peoples held in the municipality of Estancia Grande on the Costa Chica: "An official of the African and African American studies Center of the University of Texas, of African descent herself, told the participants at the meeting in Estancia Grande, Oaxaca, to give her their family names, as she, from the United States, would inform them about their African origin."

For almost a whole decade (1980-1990), the "black" question was gradually re-elaborated by actors and collectives in different regions. On the one hand, within the organizations they redefined fields of work in an attempt to respond to the experiences presented in many meetings, encounters and forums dedicated to raising awareness on origins, black culture and the analysis of the living conditions of the Afro-descendent population. In some cases, the organizations also responded to the fields that the organizations that supported projects required and the professionalization of fund-raising. On the other hand, the presence of academics and students of Mexican and foreign academic institutions also increased as various topics related to this area acquired more relevance. Some universities in the United States[11], interested in this subject, established closer contact with México Negro A.C. The leadership of the priest, Glyn Jemmott, in this organization facilitated contacts with institutions abroad, as he knew English, had the cultural knowledge to establish dialogues with academics associated with the subject, and showed himself to be fully identified with the struggles of the Afro-descendents. This capacity for promoting and mobilizing made it possible to establish international networks (for example, Afroamerica XXI) that provided feedback for local processes and encouraged participants to share experiences with other countries (Honduras, Chile, El Salvador, United States) and with black organizations.

At the beginning of the twenty-first century – the second moment in which the emergence of the subject is situated – initiatives began to appear around the discussion of "black" issue or to raise the ethnic flag in the projects of an ever-increasing number of organizations. In the coast of Oaxaca we can mention the Collectivo Cultural Africa (later Africa A.C.), Enlace de Pueblos, Organizaciones y Comunidades Autónomas, A.C. (EPOCA), Ecosta Yutucuii S.S.S., the Tututepec municipal council (2002), and recently Organización de Desarrollo Étnico Comunitario Afrodescendiente, A.C. (2008). On the coast of Guerrero, it was not formal organizations that emerged but three municipal councils that took the initiative (not by popular demand) to define themselves up as "Afro-Mexican:" the Councils of Cuajinicuilapa, Juchitán, and Copala (2008). The declaration was legally based on the autonomous character of the municipality to draw up laws and edicts on policing and good government. Various leaders of the organizations cited had previous organizational experience in a number of areas: cultural promotion, human rights, sustainable development, production and sports.

The motivation of these leader and collectives to make headway on the "black" issue varied. Amongst them we can find the opportunity to continue and strengthen the fields in which they had already been working, an interest in a new issue that could open up possibilities for accessing public funds by claiming their rights as an ethnic group, and in other cases the topic appeared due to circumstance, driven by eternal agents due to the emergence or interest in the case.

Also, the reception of the Internet in the Costa Chica made it possible to build "networks" and have access to information that increased contacts with universities, academics, organizations and sources of funding. This means of communication established itself as a scenario for interconnection on different scales that today make it possible to build transnational networks of and with black movements in America. This is revealed in the changes in discourse that now not only evoke "cultural features" as the basis for ethnic recognition but also, make use of other political instruments such as the agreements derived from the Durban Conference, the WTO Agreement 169 and references to the struggles of the Afro-descendent population in the United States and Latin America.

Some leaders of black organizations that are recognized for their political careers in black movements on an international level have visited the Costa Chica and participated in different ways in the construction of "black" culture in the region. Celeo Álvarez, one of the most visible Afro-American leaders in transnational spaces (see Agudelo, in this volume), was a force behind the creation, in 2008, of the Organización de Desarrollo Étnico Comunitario Afrodescendiente A.C. on the Costa Chica in Oaxaca. The mission of this organization is the defense of the human rights of the Afro-descendent communities, an objective inspired by previous training in human rights in La Ceiba, Honduras in which two members of the newly formed organization on the Costa Chica.[12] Another presence that motivated the efforts of the organizations was the participation of the Afro-Colombian leader, Carlos Rua, a member of the organization Ecotambor.[13] The presentation of the experience of Afro-Colombian mobilization to achieve recognition oriented the contents of ethnicity in political and legal terms. Also, it emphasized the struggle against discrimination as well as the defense of cultural and natural diversity.

This is demonstrated in one of his interventions in the Foro "Afromexicano," held in June 2007:

> There are sanctions for States for not including the question (in the census) about African descent and States are being careful.... The first thing to do is to test international public opinion with respect to demands on the Mexican State to get recognition of diversity included in the count, because if it is not, the State will be sanctioned, there are sanctions with economic repercussions, that have to do with the banks, with the multilateral banks.... Do not lose hope of finding out the possibilities of being in the 2010 census. The Mexican State is going through a period of fragile legitimacy and this is a propitious scenario... and the best legitimacy is that of the historically excluded. And the historically excluded are the Afro peoples.

This discourse is also fostered by the multiple contacts with Mexican and foreign researchers and students whose visions of the black experience is framed by their own contexts, experiences of the issue and the political positions of the organizations or institutions they represent. Some researchers or government officials have even manages to establish themselves as interlocutors for the organizations. An example of this is the UNAM's Programa Universitario México Nación Multicultural (PMNM) that at present has a number of research and promotion projects some communities on the coast of Oaxaca. Amongst these projects is the application of a census (pilot) of the Afro-descendent population aimed at showing the Instituto Nacional de Estadística, Geografía e Informática (INEGI) the pertinence of taking this population into account in the next national count. This initiative is one of the PUMNM's sets of projects, which is translated into carrying out formal work and assigning funds to this end.

The following comments show the type of contacts and referents the organizations on the Costa Chica have at their disposal:

> For the radio program "The Forgotten Root" we are planning first to talk about history, we have to begin there... We are not experts on the subject; we are now making a list of people who can help us with their opinions or a program. I am referring to researchers from the UNAM; UAM; CIESAS, the leaders of black organizations to give us their point of view on the subject and how they see things (Leader of the radio project in Tututepec, Estereo Lluvia, February, 2008).

Similarly, other officials form institutions like the Consejo Nacional para Prevenir la Discriminación (Conapred), have established themselves as interlocutors for some regional organizations in order to make agreements with government agencies. Officials from Conapred have expressed their support in public meetings and events for actions in favor of the recognition of the Afro-descendent population in this country, as an initiative aimed at extending their rights and opportunities that are at present limited by discrimination. The legal basis for such actions are to be found in the constitutional changes (2002) where the right to be free of all forms of discrimination is established as an individual right and in the international commitments that the Mexican Government has established with United Nations (UN) to attend to the Afro-descendent population (see Torres y Ramírez 2008).

Other actions of Conapred have to do with generating more knowledge on the subject of the Afro-descendent population. With this aim, it has provided funding for two projects carried out by the applied research area of the Instituto de Investigaciones Jurídicas in the UNAM.[14] These research projects again reinforce the characterization of the Afro-descendent population by their African cultural traits: carrying objects on their head, carrying a child astraddle, dialect form of Spanish, dances, poetry, and corridos, amongst other distinguishing "racial" characteristics. They even revert to old stereotypes used to identify "the black race:" boisterous, friendly, sporty, strong and cheerful (see Flores 2007). This study suggests collecting census data in order to formulate public policy to improve the economic and social conditions of these populations. It also privileges the narrative of local actors without questioning the categories used; it does not contextualize them within the power relations and in relation to their interactions with other populations.

To the actions of Conapred, I should add the interest on the part other state and federal institutions to approach the subject of the Afro-descendent population in Mexico.[15] The Comisión para el Desarrollo del los Pueblos Indígenas (CDI) in the state of Guerrero is interested in the question of the Afro-descendent population due to the demand for funds by the municipalities mentioned above that declared themselves "Afro-Mexican" municipalities. According to information provided by one of the leaders on the Costa Chica in Guerrero who says he is Afro-Mexican, at present there are conditions favorable to push for the recognition of this population, as the officials who recently look over the direction of the CDI in the state are sensitive to the topic and are more knowledgeable about the issue. There is also willingness on the part of municipal authorities and there is also the possibility that other municipalities in Guerrero will declare themselves Afro-Mexican.

Another initiative in favor of the "recognition of the Afro-Mexican population" in the country and its inclusion in national statistics is one promoted by Heladio Aguirre at present a senator in the national Senate who, in 2006, presented the project to reform by decree the Ley de la Comisión Nacional para el Desarrollo de los Pueblos Indígenas and the Ley Federal de las Entidades Paraestatales (*Gaceta del Senado, 2006*). The senator's arguments were based on the studies by Aguirre Beltrán, done in the middle of the twentieth century, but his proposal did not mention the international instruments committing the Mexican government to carry out actions in favor of the Afro-descendent population or to respond to collective demands in different regions of the country. This project had the support of various senators. However, there were no agreements to carry through the corresponding laws.

Even now, there is no census or criteria that officially define the Afro-descendent population, nor specific policies to do so; in the same way that there is no consensus on the representations on what is "black" in Mexico – nor in the region (Hoffmann 2007b). However, in general the conceptions around "black" are still permeated with stereotypes. The identification categories that until now seem to stand out most forcibly in the discourses or regional actors and even in various studies are racial references, based on physical appearance, the "naturalization" of the identity-space and characteristic cultural forms of expression. These categories attempt to construct identity markers as specific referents for the social group in question, but at the same time leave out the surrounding cultural wealth, living along side and interaction with other indigenous and mestizo social groups that also forms part of their cultural specificity. For the same reason they also omit the forms of cultural creation and re-creation as well as their capacity for exchange or adaptation to the dilemmas of globalization or the cultural systems they share.

As I have tried to demonstrate, the process of constructing the meaning of "black," is mediated by the referents of the setting in which the ethno-political actions take place, the personal experience of the actors whose social capital places them in certain levels and positions within the networks they establish and through the multicultural discourses promoted by state governments. All the spaces and places in which the Afro-descendent participants of the regional organizations participate and the people they interact through different media make up "threads" with which they weave new concepts of blackness. There are different interpretations and readings with respect to their specificities. In this way, the circulation of ideas, discourses and practices that move through the different channels favors mutual exchange and influence, the appropriation of the discourse of the Afro-descendent movement, and the production and circulation of identification categories. The multiple intersections of the referents influence how this emerging ethnicity is projected and pose serious problems for its construction.

Conclusion

The question of the Afro-descendent populations is acquiring a new dimension in the country, due to organized collective action around demands for ethnic recognition and presence in different national and international forums. We find them participating in academic meetings, in multiple references on *web* sites that talk about the subject, in the establishing of networks and interconnection with Afro-descendent movements, and even presentation of cultural expressions such as regional dances, music and poetry in touristic festivals, and urban spaces around the country where "the Afro-Mexican culture" and expressions of "blackness" are displayed. The figure presented on the following page gives us a more precise idea of present organizational dynamics.

On the other hand, the state, through its institutions, is carrying out actions that contribute it the "ethnicization of the Afro-descendent population. The willingness of the Mexican government to approach the subject of Afro-descendants is, to a certain extent, a response to the fulfillment of international political agreements, but is also a strategy oriented towards reducing the emphasis on class-based policies, as has been pointed out by a number of specialists on the subject of multiculturalism" (Hale 2005). This strategy draws attention away from the question of racism and discrimination and centers it on a policy of cultural difference that attends specific demands. This seems to be convenient for the present Mexican government, whose legitimacy has been questionable from the start.

Table 5.1: Social actors that participate in the construction of being "black" on the Costa Chica.

REGION/STATE	ORGANIZATIONS IN THE REGION	PRINCIPAL OBJECTIVES	GOVERNMENT OR EDUCATIONAL INSTITUTIONS	INTERNATIONAL ORGANIZATIONS/INSTITUTIONS	LEGISLATION
Costa Chica, Pacífico Sur	México Negro A.C.	Community and cultural development of the black villages	Programa Universitario "México Nación Multicultural", UNAM.		*Recognition as an ethnic Group in the estate.
	Alianza para el Fortalecimiento de las Regiones Indígenas y Comunidades Afromexicanas (AFRICA)	Promotion and dissemination of Black culture	Consejo Nacional para Prevenir la Discriminación (Conapred)	ODECO (Honduras)	
Oaxaca	ECOSTA YUTUCUII S.S.S.	Sustainable development	Área de Investigación Aplicada y Opinión, Instituto de Investigaciones Jurídicas, UNAM	Asociación de Universidades Negras en E.U.	* Law on Rights of indigenous peoples and communities in Oaxaca (1998)
	Enlace de Pueblos y Organizaciones y Comunidades Autónomas, A.C. (EPOCA)	Social Management			
	Organización de Desarrollo Étnico Comunitario Afrodescendiente, A.C. (ODECA)	Human Rights and community development	Programa de Desarrollo Integral de las Culturas Indígenas y Afromestizas (PRODICIA). Dirección General de Culturas Populares. Secretaría de Cultura		

Table 5.1 (cont)

REGION/ STATE	ORGANIZATIONS IN THE REGION	PRINCIPAL OBJECTIVES	GOVERNMENT OR EDUCATIONAL INSTITUTIONS	INTERNATIONAL ORGANIZATIONS/ INSTITUTIONS	LEGIS- LATION
Guerrero	Museo Comunitario Cuijla, A. C.	Extension of Afro-Mexican culture	Instituto Nacional de Antro-pología		None
			Programa Tercera Raíz, Direc-ción Gral. de Culturas Populares, CONACULTA		
			CDI, Delegación Guerrero		
			Instituto de Cultura de Guerrero		
			Ángel Aguirre Rivero, Senador de la República (Legislatura)		
			Municipal governments of Cua-jinicuilapa, Juchitán y Copala		

Notes

1. Translated by Susan L. Jones Harris.

2. The results are presented in full in my doctoral thesis "Política, espacio y construcción social del poder local-regional en la Costa Chica de Oaxaca", CIESAS, México, D.F., 2008.

3. That is to say, the representation presented in the media and national education.

4. The category "people of reason" refers to a concept ascribed in the inter-ethnic relation. There are divisions that define superior and inferior categories expressed in dichotomies indian/mestizo or people of custom/people of reason. In this organization of the world the condition of inferiority is associated with the indigenous population.

5. For the case of the Afro-descendent population on the Costa Chica, see the studies by Aguirre Beltrán (1958) and Flanet (1977). For an analysis of the academic production on the subject, see Hoffmann (2006) and Hoffmann (2007).

6. In Oaxaca there are a large number of foundations and cooperation organizations that support local and regional initiatives attending to the indigenous population. It is perceived as one of the states in Mexico with the greatest ethnic diversity and where a multicultural, unique in the country, is pursued.

7. The information used to write this section was collected during stays over different periods (between 2004-2008), the last one as part of the "Afrodesc" project.

8. These interests were related to personal experience, local leaderships that were taken up in the locality or region, social capital and resources available to work on this issue.

9. For more a more detailed account, see the work of Hoffmann (2007). The author explains two ethnic models on the Costa Chica that refer to "representations directly linked to local contexts and to specific configurations of domination and power, that are translated into spaces and relations between social groups the regional differences being labeled by their identities" and to discursive elaborations of multi-ethnicity by the formations in the state in which the societies are immersed.

10. The concept of popular culture is close to the theoretical perspective conceived by Guillermo Bonfil (1982, cited in Pérez,

1999). Bonfil proposes the use of this concept to achieve a better understanding of cultural dynamics and the phenomenon of ethnic identity in an inter-cultural context. The author characterizes popular cultures "as those corresponding to the subordinate world in a classist and multi-ethnic society of colonial origin".

11. In particular the Association of Black Universities.

12. Celeo Álvarez is the principal leader of the Organización Desarrollo Comunitario, a black Honduran movement and is a member of the board of ONECA. In turn, ONECA participates in various Latin American organization: Alianza Estratégica Afrolatinoamericana y Caribeña, Consejo Consultivo del Sistema de la Integración Centroamericana CC-SICA, Comisión de Desarrollo Sustentable de las Naciones Unidas, member of the Foro Permanente de la Sociedad Civil de la Comisión Centroamericana de Ambiente y Desarrollo del Sistema de Integración Centroamericana and participated in the National Alliance of Latino and Caribbean Communities, USA.

13. Ecotambor is an Afro-Colombian organization the objective of which is "to work for the promotion of the rights of ethnic groups in Colombia, with emphasis on the right to information, justice and the development of alternative inter-ethnic communication. One of the main lines of action is the promote access to the mass media by ethnic groups and the creation of their own media" (http://www.comminit.com/es/node/44165/print). Consulted, November 2008.

14. See Proyecto 2006 by Julia Flores: "Afrodescendientes en México: Reconocimiento y propuestas para evitar la discriminación" and Proyecto 2007 (by the same author): "Procesos de construcción de identidad, condición de vida y discriminación en comunidades afrodescendientes en los estados de Coahuila y Tamaulipas", Conapred. There is an article on the Afro-descendent question in the publication coordinated by Alejandra Becerra (2008), also published by Conapred.

15. Recently, officials of the Dirección General de Población in the estate of Oaxaca went on a field trip to obtain more information on the Afro-descendent population of the Costa Chica and the community of Valerio Trujano, located in the district of Cuicatlán, Oaxaca. The institution's 4 monthly publication for January-April dedicated one of its numbers to the subject of the Afro-descendent population in the afore mentioned regions.

Bibliography

Agudelo, Carlos. 2005. *Retos del multiculturalismo en Colombia. Política y poblaciones negras.* Medellín: IEPRI/IRD/ICANH/La Carreta.

Aguirre Beltrán, Gonzalo.1984 [1946]. *La población negra de México.* México: Fondo de Cultura Económica.

Bartolomé, Miguel Alberto. 1997. *Gente de costumbre, gente de razón. Las identidades étnicas en México.* México: Editorial Siglo XXI.

Flores, Julia. 2007. *Procesos de construcción de identidad, condición de vida y discriminación en las comunidades afrodescendientes en los estados de Coahuila y Tamaulipas.* México: Conapred.

Gaceta del Senado. 2006. LX Legislatura, Un año de ejercicio, primer periodo ordinario n° 7, jueves 26 de octubre de 2006.

Giménez, Gilberto. 2000. Identidades étnicas: estado de la cuestión. In *Los retos de la etnicidad en los estados-nación del siglo XXI,* coord. Leticia Reina. México: CIESAS/INI/Porrúa, 45-70.

Greene, Shane. 2007. Entre lo indio, lo negro y lo incaico: The Spatial Hierarchies of Difference in Multicultural Peru. *The Journal of Latin American and Caribbean Anthropology* 12(2): 441-474.

Hale, Charles. 2005. Identidades politizadas, derechos culturales y las nuevas formas de gobierno en la época neoliberal". In *Memorias del mestizaje. Cultura política en Centroamérica de 1920 al presente,* eds Darío Euraque, Jeffrey Gould y Charles Hale. Guatemala: CIRMA: 19-51.

Hoffmann, Odile. 2007a. Frateros y criollos, blancos y negros en la Costa Chica. El 'lugar' y el 'capital espacial' en la reproducción de la diferencia. In *Retos de la diferencia. Los actores de la multiculturalidad entre México y Colombia,* eds Odile Hoffmann y Teresa Rodríguez. México: CEMCA/CIESAS/IRD: 363-397.

Hoffmann, Odile. 2007b. De las 'tres razas' al mestizaje: diversidad de las representaciones colectivas acerca de lo 'negro' en México (Veracruz y Costa Chica). *Diario de campo. Suplemento* 42: 98-107.

Hoffmann, Odile. 2006. Negros y afromestizos en México: viejas y nuevas lecturas de un mundo olvidado. *Revista Mexicana de Sociología,* año 68 (1):103-135, Enero-Marzo.

Jenkins, Richard. 1997. *Rethinking Ethnicity. Arguments and Explorations.* Londres: Sage Publications.

Lara Millán, Gloria. 2007. El recurso de la diferencia étnico-racial en las lógicas de inclusión política. El caso de Pinotepa Nacional Oaxaca. In *Retos de la diferencia. Los actores de la multiculturalidad entre México y Colombia*, eds Odile Hoffmann y María Teresa Rodríguez. México: CEMCA/CIESAS/IRD: 81-110.

Motta, J. 2006. Tras la heteroidentificación. El "movimiento negro" costachiquense y la selección de marbetes étnicos. *Dimensión Antropológica* 38: 115-118. Revista en línea, consulta realizada el 1 de noviembre de 2008.

Naveda, Adriana. 1999. Fuentes para el estudio de la población esclava en México. *América Latina en la historia económica. Boletín de fuentes* 12: 63-69.

Ng'weno, Bettina. 2007. Can Ethnicity Replace Race? Afro-Colombians, Indigeneity and the Colombian Multicultural State. *The Journal of Latin American and Caribbean Anthropology* 12(2): 414-440.

Pepin Lehalleur, Marielle. 2003. ¿Existe el regionalismo popular? In *Territorios, actores y poder. Regionalismos emergentes en México*. México: Universidad de Guadalajara/Universidad Autónoma de Yucatán: 25-48.

Pérez Maya, Lorena. 1999. Aportaciones de Guillermo Bonfil al concepto de lo popular. *Nueva Antropología. Revista de Ciencias Sociales* 55: 89-103.

Restrepo, Eduardo. 2007. El 'giro al multiculturalismo' desde un encuadre afro-indígena. *The Journal of Latin American and Caribbean Anthropology* 12(2): 475-485.

Rinaudo, Christian. 2010. Más allá de la 'identidad negra': mestizaje y dinámicas raciales en la ciudad de Veracruz. In *Mestizaje y diferencia. Políticas y culturas de "lo negro" alrededor del Caribe*, ed Elisabeth Cunin. México: INAH/UNAM/CEMCA/IRD.

Torres, Jorge e Isidro Ramírez. 2008. Aportaciones para la visibilidad, la no discriminación y el reconocimiento de los pueblos afromexicanos en la Costa Chica de Oaxaca, México. In *Atención a la discriminación en Iberoamérica. Un recuento inicial*, coord. Alejandro Becerra. México: Consejo Nacional para Prevenir la Discriminación: 219-241.

Velásquez, María E. y Odile Hoffmann. 2007. Investigaciones sobre africanos y afrodescendientes en México: acuerdos y consideraciones desde la historia y la antropología. *Diario de campo* 91: 62-69.

Chapter 6

Mestizaje and Ethnicity in the City of Veracruz, Mexico[1]

Christian Rinaudo

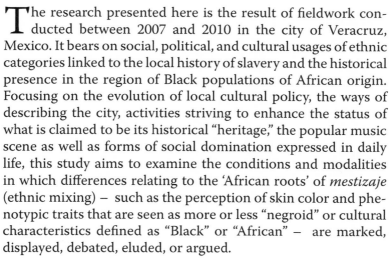

The research presented here is the result of fieldwork conducted between 2007 and 2010 in the city of Veracruz,
Mexico. It bears on social, political, and cultural usages of ethnic
categories linked to the local history of slavery and the historical
presence in the region of Black populations of African origin.
Focusing on the evolution of local cultural policy, the ways of
describing the city, activities striving to enhance the status of
what is claimed to be its historical "heritage," the popular music
scene as well as forms of social domination expressed in daily
life, this study aims to examine the conditions and modalities
in which differences relating to the 'African roots' of *mestizaje*
(ethnic mixing) – such as the perception of skin color and phenotypic traits that are seen as more or less "negroid" or cultural
characteristics defined as "Black" or "African" – are marked,
displayed, debated, eluded, or argued.

Several elements motivated the choice of the city of Veracruz for this study. So far, most research on Afro-Mexican
studies has concerned places that had long remained isolated
and whose inhabitants displayed cultural and phenotypic

traits easily attributable to their "African origins" (Costa Chica between the States of Guerrero and Oaxaca, villages like Coyolillo in the State of Veracruz). These are now well known, of interest to both scholars working on "populations of African origin" and militants involved in the process of recognition of "Black identity" in Mexico, often in connection with international organizations. Although such political, cultural and social projects, which help increase the degree of awareness of belonging to a group ("Afro-Mexicans"), may in themselves be an interesting subject for research that is beginning to be addressed (Lara Millán 2008, Lewis 2000), they do not account for other social usages among categories referring to their African heritage in contemporary and urban Mexico.[2] These usages appear in historical processes of transformation of representations of mestizaje and regional identities, but also emerge in concrete situations as observed in urban areas where the ethnic dimension is not always present and may acquire different meanings according to context, ranging from prestige to stigma.

Despite its long history as a port for bringing in and trading in African slaves and the process of political recognition of the importance of African roots in local culture, there are today in the city of Veracruz no collective activities aiming to develop awareness of belonging to a single social group self-identified as "Black" or "Afro-descendant", nor are there any organizations that seek to speak or take action on behalf of people of African origin. Here, the idea of the existence of a specific group, like "Afro-Veracruzans" or a "Black community of Veracruz," has little meaning in an urban space where the inhabitants identify themselves largely on the basis of class distinctions or regional differences. The term *Jarocho*, referring, often indiscriminately, to people from the South of the State, the *Sotavento* coast and the city of Veracruz, relates more to the issue of *mestizaje*, or even "specific *mestizaje*" and its different roots than to Black identity, even if it did evoke, at one time in local history, the Black rural population in the southern State of Veracruz (Delgado Calderón 2004). Moreover, somatic variations among inhabitants (skin color, morphology, facial features) are unimportant, which may cause confusion among "Black" militants when they come to Veracruz in search of a "Black population" sharing their condition. True, another characteristic of urban life in Mexico is surely the constant use of qualifiers referring to *mestizaje* and somatic and cultural differences (*Indígena, Mestizo, Creollo, Moreno, Pardo, Negro, Mulato, Güero,* etc), even if there are few visible differences in terms of distinctive features.

An empirical approach

This study adopted the inductive non-substantialist approach now shared by many researchers working in this field[3] and refrained from presupposing the presence of existing entities. It considers the matter of Afro-descent as one factor among others for understanding: the broader processes of racism and discrimination; maintenance of ethnic boundaries and ethnicization processes; empowerment phenomena and the development of militant organizations; the stakes of patrimonialization and construction of collective memory; the emergence of multicultural policies and redefinitions of citizenship; "ethnic" or "non-ethnic" framing of events and specific courses of action; and moments when specific identities crystallize.

In this perspective, the survey work involved studying the moments, modalities and reasons for which ethnic boundaries are marked, maintained, signified, proclaimed, disclaimed, or valued. The ethnographic approach adopted bears on: contexts or moments of more or less strong expression of "groupness"[4] definable in cultural terms; on the social uses of categories referring to color or presumed African origin; on civic organizations involved in processes of patrimonialization of an urban memory of slavery and *mestizaje*; on enhancing the "Third Root" in defining cultural policy; and on social actors who, especially in the cultural field, emphasize the city's "African roots" and its place in the Caribbean, as well as individual and collective staging of to relationships with Africa, the Caribbean and the "Black Atlantic." Special attention has also been granted to dealing with physical appearance, gait, dance, and dress inspired by globalized, re-localized models that could be identified as "Black culture" – whether or not this has led to any cultural movement (promotion of Black music and Afro dances) or identity claims (demand for recognition by entrepreneurs of "Black identity") that are specifically, continually or unanimously labeled as "Black" or "Afro-descendant."

Thus, the hypothesis guiding this approach is that such phenomena, sometimes insubstantial or inconsequent in certain situations, actually have a major role in maintaining ethnic boundaries. The political changes in the past twenty years contributed to orienting research towards collective forms of action aiming to produce or crystallize ethnic solidarity by relying on cultural (sharing common attributes) or political bases (sharing a common condition of being minimized or victims of racial discrimination). However, the ethnicization processes underway in certain regions do not account for the space, time, and fields in which ethnic categories - often created in the colonial period - express themselves and are transformed, and in which some distinctions are reinforced while others fade or appear more flexible and sometimes less necessary. Besides cases where awareness of identities develops against the ideology of *mestizaje* and its principles of indifference to differences that deny social inequality and ethnic discrimination, other relationships between *mestizaje* and ethnicity can be observed that also have their social importance. For example, relations that develop in the city involve the power balance and forms of domination on the basis of distinctions constantly noted and reproduced between on the one hand light-skinned, well- dressed 'beautiful people' (*gente bonita*) who live in residential areas, dine in expensive restaurants and go to fashionable discotheques, and on the other hand poor people, 'Indians', 'Black', peasants or workers. Guillermo Bonfil made mention of this schism between 'imaginary Mexico' (modern, urban, cosmopolitan, heir of the Spanish conquest) and '*México profundo*' (Bonfil Batalla, 1990). Once again, the relationship between *mestizaje* and ethnicity constantly means thinking, justifying, reasserting the idea of *mestizaje* and describing and structuring its different 'roots' and associated 'populations'.

To account for the heuristic value of this approach, three orientations will be presented for this research referring to three distinct levels of analysis: one bearing on social and socially situated activities that entail 'describing the city'; another aiming to account for definitions and transformations of localized cultural policy; and a third highlighting modes of expression, displaying and experimenting with 'elective Africanity' in urban public space.

The tourist discourse around the city

Veracruz, one of the main ports for reaching the continent or departing towards other destinations, was not spared the social phenomenon represented throughout the 19th century by the passage of foreign travellers and chroniclers visiting Latin America. There are many written traces of descriptions of the region and its inhabitants, most of which were published in a collection of eleven works, coordinated by Martha Poblett Miranda under the title *Cien viajeros en Veracruz. Crónicas y relatos* (Poblett Miranda 1992). These travel diaries have already been amply commented and analyzed,[5] recreating a picture of Veracruz seen at the time above all as a dangerous inhospitable unwholesome town, a dismal place that was hard to reach, whose local population was often described as indolent, 'sleeping all day in frightful sunshine', and belonging 'to all Mexican races, their colour ranging from ochre to ebony' (García Díaz 2002, 215-238).

The development of tourism as such did not begin until the 1920s-1930s, when yellow fever ceased to be perceived as a threat and with the arrival from Europe and the United States of a sport-loving hygienist movement that hailed the benefits of bathing in the sea and sunshine (García Díaz 1998, 48). It was also at this time, with the arrival in Veracruz of several railways, the modernisation of urban transport, the increasingly widespread use of electricity and the will to make Veracruz a tourist destination, that there was the revitalization of Carnival, thought to date from the 17th century. Taken up by social clubs, and shopkeepers and hotel associations who were funded by the municipality and the Veracruz State government, the aim was to attract more visitors to the city and transform this Carnival into a popular media event of national and international renown (Guadarrama Olivera 2002).

At the end of the 1930s and in the early 1940s, Miguel Alemán Valdés, then governor of the State of Veracruz before becoming President of Mexico in 1946, stimulated the development of tourism in the region, inciting investors from the capital to buy land and build tourist infrastructures, like Hotel Mocambo described today as an ideal place 'for the rich and famous who enjoyed staying in places full of romance and tranquility'.[6] This was precisely the type of clientele targeted by one of the State of Veracruz's first tourist guides, published in 1940 by the Mexican Tourism Association and the Department of Tourism of the *Gobernación* Secretariat. This guidebook proposed an itinerary called 'Travel in the land of flowers', from Mexico City to Veracruz.

On reaching the coast, a chapter titled 'Rejoicing in Veracruz' clearly emphasizes the entertainment typical of seaside tourism and describes the town through the special atmosphere prevailing there, in a setting characterized by both its colonial charm and its modern infrastructures (Anonymous 1940). The many photographs illustrating the text include, on the one hand, stereotypic representations of a happy local population — *Jarochos* — singing, playing music or dancing, who, as Ricardo Pérez Montfort clearly showed at the time of post-revolutionary nationalism, gradually moved away from the connotation of poverty and peasantry, as well as relations with an African heritage, to highlight a whitened image evoking aristocratic ascent in terms of skin colour, posture and dress (Pérez Montfort 2007, 200). On the other hand, the photographs in this guidebook also show tourists in swimsuits and clothing fashionable among urban upper and middle classes visiting the coast to enjoy the merry festive atmosphere, tropical climate and bathing in the sea in an idyllic setting of fine sand, palm trees and lively terraces by the sea.

Thus, the guide develops a vision of tropical coasts seen from Mexico. Stripped of any mention of African presence or indigenous roots, not yet stamped as part of the Caribbean cultural area, it was then entirely dedicated to satisfying the whims of wealthy refined 'modern' summer visitors from the capital.

It is in this context that the city of Veracruz is often described as a tourist destination, a place to 'have a good time', 'have fun,' 'make merry.' And this 'specificity' of the port as a place one visits - for its 'joyous nature' attributed to its inhabitants' ancestral roots - contributed to the stereotypes attributed to the local population, something widely 'overplayed' by the inhabitants themselves to foreigners, and by professionals who earned their living from this urban folklore, especially around the city's main square (Flores Martos 2004).

Thus, in contemporary travel guides, agency brochures, online presentations and other advertising material vaunting the merits of the place, the first thing that appears from now on is the association, explicit or implicit, between the festive, merry, convivial, rowdy definition of Veracruz and its inhabitants, its identification with the Caribbean and the contribution of cultural, physical and psychological traits inherited from the African presence highlighted to describe the specificity of this old colonial town. For example, the *Guide Bleu*, a French reference for upscale cultural tourism, insists on the commercial importance of the colonial port and the character of its inhabitants: "Its inhabitants, the *Jarochos*, of mixed Spanish, Indian and African descent, display a gaiety they demonstrate more specifically during Carnival, one of the most brilliant after those of Rio de Janeiro and Trinidad." (*Guide Bleu* 2005)

Similarly, in the *Guide du Routard*, published by the same press group, Hachette, and targeting French tourists through a more laid-back vision of cultural tourism (carrying rucksacks, staying with local people...), the description focuses above all on the charm, exciting nightlife and tropical hedonism of the place and the local population: "There isn't much to see in Veracruz, but the city has a certain charm, with its squares lined with palm trees and its Promenade on the *malecón* (boardwalk) along the port. A hot ambiance reigns around the Zócalo after sunset and way into the night. This is the city of music and dance (Afro-Cuban influence)." (*Guide du Routard* 2006)

Paradoxically, while tourism is above all a national phenomenon in Mexico — especially Veracruz — as in many Latin American countries (Raymond 2004), there are still few national guidebooks. In an online guide titled *Travel By Mexico, All About Mexico*, the introductory chapter on Veracruz describes the town

145

as the cradle of the Mexican nation, emphasising the 'mixing of two worlds,' Spanish and Indian, the 'cultural diversity' — which, in Mexico, refers essentially to the diversity of Indian cultures — and the joyous nature of the inhabitants, the *Jarochos*.[7]

If national descriptions emphasize that Veracruz is a historic center for the meeting of two worlds, a local thematic guide dedicated to the culture of *Son* (sound) presents a more complex landscape in which the different influences have to do with the different roots of *mestizaje* and cultural features from the Caribbean:

> "The culture of *Son* covers practically the entire coast of Veracruz, although notable differences appear according to region: to the North, *Son Huasteco* has a slow beat and a melancholy mood with the violin while, in Los Tuxtlas region, in the south of the State, *Son Campesino* (peasant) or *Abajeño* (coastal) is much more cheerful because of the influence of African and Caribbean culture introduced to the region." (Jiménez Illescas 2002, 6)

Concerning the city of Veracruz in particular, a historical paragraph retraces the context of the arrival of populations of African origin and their subsequent importance in the formation of local culture resulting from the *mestizaje* of 'three worlds': Spanish, Indian and African. The author of *La Ruta del Son* also insists on relations between the rural coastal area and the city and on the former's influence in what is described at the *Porteño* nature:

> "Another substantial migration is made up of sequestered persons from Africa, which forms the third ethnic root of the coast of Veracruz. Because of the dearth of native people, manpower held in slavery was brought in. These slaves were distributed from the port to perform hard labour in mines and sugarcane plantations. A century after the start of this migration, in 1681, half of the port's thousand inhabitants were Black. Erotic exchanges between Blacks and Indians produced the *Jarochos*, a term

> describing the rural population of the coastal plains
> of the *Sotavento*. And it was in *Jarocha* music, a genre
> to which this *mestizaje* gave rise, [...] that the three
> worlds present in countryside of Veracruz since
> colonial times melded. Its culture, clearly *Vaquero*
> and *Campesino*, was central to being *Porteño*."
> (Jiménez Illescas 2002, 58)

Different analytical elements may be drawn from these few examples. First, the change in the description of the 1940s and what is said today is obvious. Now, all insist on the joyous welcoming atmosphere of the coast and city, in contrast with most 19th-century travel accounts of Veracruz, like the view given by the English merchant William Bullock in 1824, as 'the most disagreeable place on earth' and 'the most unhealthy spot in the world', making 'the stranger shudder every hour he remains within its walls' (Bullock 1992, 42).

Since all tourist discourse characteristically highlights the destination's assets, the assets in this case have been, quite consistently since it arose in the 1930s-1940s, the fun, the friendly festive atmosphere, the people's joy of living, described as elements central to the destination's appeal. But it is only recently that this local characteristic of the city and coastal region is described by highlighting the *mestizaje* of the population, the diversity of its origins, the African and Afro-Cuban influences linked to the history of slavery and cultural movements in the Caribbean, as well as the resulting wealth of forms of expression.

African roots and Caribbean insertion in cultural policy

Another research orientation entails studying social rationales having contributed in Veracruz to valuing 'Afro-Caribbean' culture and understanding the institutional, academic and partisan stakes involved in its inclusion in local cultural policy.

In his work on Mexican popular culture and nationalist stereotypes, Ricardo Pérez Montfort, who studied the *Jarocho Fandango* and its cultural position of the 'Afro-Andalusian Caribbean' in the 17th to 19th centuries, clearly shows how the construction of national cultural symbols entailed downplaying regional diversity in the 1920s-1930s in Mexico (Pérez Montfort 2003). The 1970s-1980s marked the end of this post-revolutionary period and centralist homogenizing cultural nationalism (Jiménez, 2006). This was the start of a cultural decentralization process initiated by the federal administration and gradually instituted in all Mexican States, Secretariats, Institutes and Councils for Culture.

Thus, the years following the creation, in 1987, of the *Instituto Veracruzano de la Cultura* (IVEC) gave rise to a definition of the main orientations and implementation of what was to be a decentralized cultural policy in the State of Veracruz. Three elements are of interest here because they profoundly marked what can be analysed as a 'Caribbean' and 'Afro-Caribbean' flavor to the cultural policy of Veracruz.

The first entailed, from the creation of IVEC, institutionalizing work begun at the end of the 1970s for the retrieval and diffusion of *Son Jarocho* as the 'authentic musical tradition of Veracruz' and *Fandango* as 'the region's traditional community celebration.' This movement that initially aimed to be a return to the rural Afro-Andalusian Caribbean tradition described by Antonio García de León (García de León 1992) contributed to producing a new cultural and artistic style that, though very different from the past reality it sought, created new ties with this cultural area, introducing or reintroducing Caribbean instruments and blending the rhythmic, instrumental and harmonic bases of *Son Jarocho* and Afro-Caribbean music (García de León 2006, 58). In so doing, musical experimentation, exchange and the circulation of knowledge made possible by the intensification of meetings and festivals revealed made the different influences of this music more visible and audible, in particular those from Africa.

Another element marking local cultural policy impelled by IVEC in the first years of its existence was the work of relaunching in the city of Veracruz *Danzón* and *Son Montuno*[8], two styles of dance and music of Cuban origin introduced in the late 19th and early 20th centuries thanks to permanent contacts between the ports of Havana and Veracruz, but also to the presence of a small Cuban community, which probably facilitated their very rapid adoption in lower-class neighborhoods and in public places in Veracruz to the point of becoming of the city's main attractions, mentioned in all tourist guides. At the time of IVEC's creation, the *Danzón* tradition in Veracruz was waning, the golden age of *Son Montuno* was a thing of the past with many bands and musicians having moved to Mexico City to pursue their careers and eke out a living from their music. This is how one of the first measures taken was to ask those in charge of cultural promotion to locate the musicians and groups of that time to offer them new possibilities for a career in the city. It was from this project begun in the 1980s that several major events, including the Festival Internacional Afrocaribeño, then Festival Internacional Agustín Lara and Festival del Son Montuno, were created a few years later.

The third element in this cultural policy was precisely that of stimulating academic reflection on the Caribbean and its African heritage, which led to creating the Festival Internacional Afrocaribeño. It started with the organization of two academic forums in 1989 and 1990: *Veracruz también es Caribe.*[9] The purpose of these meetings was to present research results to promote a representation of Veracruz as a region culturally turned towards the Caribbean. At the same time, there were similar dynamics in Cancún, Quintana Roo, with what was called the International Caribbean Cultural Festival in 1988. But what would actually become a characteristic of the cultural policy of Veracruz was the association of this regional identification with the Caribbean and a national program also launched in 1989 under the name *Nuestra Tercera Raíz* (Our Third Root). Its goal was to study and add value to the African presence in Mexico by recognising it as the Third Root in the formation of the country's '*mestizo* culture'. It led to the realisation of specific research, exhibitions, symposia and workshops, as well as the organization of National Afro-Americanist meetings. This combination of a definition of local cultural policy focusing both on the positioning of Veracruz in the 'Caribbean cultural basin' and on awareness on a local level of the national 'Our Third Root' program largely resulted from the presence and commitment of Luz María Martínez Montiel at the head of the Cultural Heritage at IVEC at the time of its foundation. She was in charge of renovation of the City Museum with the first display dedicated to slavery in a Mexican museum, while also coordinating the 'Our Third Root' program for the Dirección General de Culturas Populares. On the one hand, the Caribbean dimension of Veracruz developed around other rationales in its recent history, in particular the growth of festive and sexual tourism not directly linked to the Third Root issue and focusing on the cultural heritage from the Caribbean area. From this standpoint, this dimension is not strictly local in that it is part of tourist and heritage policy aiming to identify the east coast of Mexico with this regional area, positioning places of entertainment and cultural interest in a highly competitive international market. On the other hand, the program focusing on the Third Root of *mestizaje* is more strictly national and does not correspond to rationales of tourist appeal. In this context, it is interesting to see how, at any given time, valuing the Caribbean dimension and the theme of the Third Root converge in Veracruz, in the context of implementation of local cultural policy. And it is precisely following this consideration begun by the IVEC Caribbean Studies Centre and for the fourth National Afro-Americanist meeting organized in June 1994 in the city of Veracruz that this convergence was reinforced thanks to the first International Afro-Caribbean Festival.

Consequently, this Festival results from the implementation of cultural policy that itself results from academic discussions conducted in this key period in the history of Mexico and Latin America in which issues relating to diversity, multiculturalism, the cultural heritage, decentralization and cultural globalization emerged in the debates and public agendas. This policy entailed bringing together various orientations that began to emerge, in both academic research and public action. The former aimed to study the African cultural heritage in Latin America. Directly linked to Luz María Martínez Montiel's influence, it arose from political and academic interest specifically focusing on the history of slavery. It was a matter of promoting the Third Root of *mestizaje*, the historic contribution of slaves and descendants of slaves to Mexican national culture.

A second orientation present in the issue of defining and implementing local cultural policy is borne by researchers close to militant Afro-Mexican movements (Cruz Carretero 2005) in connection with Black Studies departments in North American universities. In this case, it is a matter of accepting the cultural and somatic specificity linked to the African presence in Mexico, not only as a common heritage for everyone, but also as a characteristic that can be reasserted today in the context of viewing Mexico as pluriethnic with 'Afro-Mexicans' as one of the ethnic groups forming the national society.

A third orientation prevailing in Veracruz emphasizes the diversity of cultural heritage in the 'Afro-Andalusian Caribbean'. It promotes *mestizaje* as the essence of folk culture, *mestizaje* recognising the importance of the African heritage without making it exclusive. Thus, in his texts, García de León evokes the 'folk civilization' that generated *mestizaje* in the colonial period against the Spanish conquistadors and the city's white elite, a 'folk culture with various influences, African, Caribbean, European' that developed on the fringe of the dominant class's elitist culture. He presents Veracruz as the 'tropical Babel of the Indies where all possible races and mixtures coexist,' which differs from militant 'Afro-Mexican' rationales that seek to relate these traits solely to 'Black identity', as opposed to the ideology of *mestizaje* (García de León 1996).

The difficulty of maintaining these different orientations is apparent in the design of posters for the Festival. Most of them emphasize phenotypic traits and physical postures representing Africanity, which, though stylized, may seem quite remote from the very idea of the Third Root's contribution to contemporary Mexico's national *mestizo* culture.

On the other hand, after various changes at the head of IVEC, this illustration of Africanity has sometimes been replaced by another, more in stride with the focus on the many origins of *mestizaje* and cultural diversity in the Caribbean. This was the case in particular in 1999 when the Festival changed its name to Festival of the Caribbean, or in 2005 when, after restoring its original name, a subtitle was added, specifying that this was a 'Festival for everyone.' In the former case, the poster evoked the

Caribbean in a very stylised way around the letter 'C' and the sun. In the second, it sought to express diversity through the representation of a multiplicity of faces, each different from all the others.

It is possible to conclude that this policy of institutional promotion of the Third Root has not succeeded locally in creating a community feeling around Afrodescent (Sue 2007, 2009). Not particularly influential in the city of Veracruz, the position supported by Afro-Mexican militant movements has been able to develop, in a very limited way, in some of the region's villages. It is also possible to hypothesise that all those years of promoting the Third Root of Mexican *mestizaje*, punctuated by academic meetings, exhibitions and many concerts with groups invited from the entire Caribbean region performing alongside local music groups, have produced some effects. From the start, the different players involved in implementing cultural policy agreed, for example, on unequivocal criticism of the dominant position of a conservative local elite that rejected all forms of recognition of a common heritage linked to African origins and the cultural proximity of Veracruz with the Caribbean. From this standpoint, thirty years of public policy highlighting 'traditional' *Son Jarocho*, 'Afro-Caribbean' music, the Caribbean as a specific cultural area and the Third Root of *mestizaje* did bring about profound changes in the criteria for cultural legitimation. They contributed further to moving from a historical period (1930-1970) characterized by accepted negation of the African heritage and 'whitening' operations for stereotyped notions of *Jarocha* identity (Pérez Montfort 2007) at a time when African roots and *mestizaje* had become part of the representation of local society. This does not mean that this representation is accepted as such, but that it has now become a legitimate norm for defining local identity. Consequentially, the stakes for social actors in concrete situations involve positioning themselves with respect to this norm which they can accept or reject, assume or endure.

Elective Africanity and *Callejera* culture

To account for all these possible stakes, the third research orientation presented entails examining identity-related expression as it appears in public places as the stage for urban life. From this point of view, it is in the interest of many establishments – from the city of Veracruz and its historic center's pedestrian squares and streets, to nightlife establishments and the *malecón* (boardwalk) where passers-by meet - that all of these places are occupied daily by musicians and dancers, regular visitors and passing tourists who, by their very co-presence, scenically produce modes of social identification combining different levels of affiliation and social distinction, thereby making them interpretable. We will broach this issue here through an ethnographic study aiming to describe the forms of expression of 'elective Africanity'.

The study bears on a cultural program called *Noches de Callejón* (night in the streets) organized every weekend at El Portal de Miranda, a small pedestrian street in the historic center of Veracruz. This program was instigated by the artistic director, singer and guitarist of the Juventud Sonera group whose initial project was to bring back the tradition of *Son Montuno* that existed in Veracruz since the end of the 1920s and include modern elements to attract younger people (drums, electric guitar...). Thus, since the release of the recording *¡Guarachero!*[10] very close to the Afro-Cuban tradition, the group's leader has been paying more attention to his pop-star look while publically declaring his interest in *Son*. After letting his hair grow and playing electric guitars sporting prestigious American brands, he looks more and more like Jimi Hendrix, Lenny Kravitz or Ben Harper as his fans keep reminding him, thereby intensifying the references to black American culture.

Thanks to its location, at the crossroads of tourist routes and local inhabitants' evening strolls, this urban stage in Veracruz is a place where ordinary passers-by interested in the local scene can meet a group of mutual acquaintances made up of regular patrons who greet musicians as they arrive, form small social groups, start dancing and strike up conversations... This does not mean they form a homogeneous social group or a single age class. Many are between 16 and 30 years old, but there are also older individuals, alone or with partners. Some are from the city's working-class neighborhoods, while others belong to a local cultural elite who enjoy this type of music and urban atmosphere.

These regular patrons, despite differences - between young people and those who are not so young, men and women, passing dancers and musicians, give rise to a form of expression that entails sharing certain cultural elements whose codes may be subject to interpretation and signification. It is not so much a matter of defining oneself as 'Black', but of behaving 'like a Black', dancing according to certain rhythmic sequences, overplaying choreographic gestures and movements of different bodily expressions referring to the Afro-Caribbean world. Most of the time, these demonstrations are identified by the public and musicians as a 'show' that differs from more traditional dancing in couples. A circle forms gradually around the person, shouting encouragements, regular visitors exchange remarks and the musicians stray from their routine with more emphatic improvisation and solos. Some people regularly put on such 'shows', like a 20-year-old girl living in a lower-class neighbourhood of Veracruz, whose skin colour and features are not particularly 'Black' or 'mulatto', who often starts dancing when musicians play Carlos Oliva's *Pelotero a la Bola*. At the end, one of the musicians in the group always thanks her by name with a short comment like 'Look at that Black girl's wild dance!' (June 2009). According to the people interviewed on her performance, her style resembles both that of the *Rumberas* who perform in cabarets and the erotic dances practiced with table dancing stereotypically associating unbridled sexuality and Africanity.

Other people may also put on such shows, like an old lady of modest origin from Veracruz who often dances for tourists near restaurants at the Zócalo. In this case, regular patrons and musicians describe her way of dancing as 'Creole' (*Criollo*). This category is used locally to describe old rural Caribbean traditions, at the origin of *Son*, a mixture of Spanish guitar and the syncopated beats brought by African slaves. Thus, in addition to inciting admiration on the part of these knowledgeable audiences, this lady's performance is viewed as an expression of the old Afro-Caribbean heritage of Veracruz.

154

Young boys and girls from the city or region accustomed to more alternative cultural venues, but regularly present at *Noches de Callejón,* may also join in such self-display, combining emblematic signs of Caribbean Blacks (dreadlocks, beard, colour and style clothing...) and ways of moving and dancing, which, there again and in a different style, are described as forms of expression of elective Africanity. This is what is explained by a 23-year-old man from a lower-case neighbourhood of Veracruz who plays drums and sings with friends in public transportation when he needs money:

- I really enjoy coming here to El Portal in the late evening when there is a special atmosphere and everyone joins a little in the fun of showing off what's Black in you (laughs)
- Do you define yourself as Black?
- No, not at all, but we all have some Black ancestors, don't we? So, when you hear this music and you're plunged in this ambiance, you can't help but start moving in a certain way...
- Just how? Could you be more explicit?
- Not really. I don't see myself... But if you take my buddies, like Ricardo: he feels it more like a Jamaican, you see, reggaeman, easy [...]. While Fallo'll really be influenced by the rap movement, hip hop and all that [...]. Sara, my girlfriend, lets loose with African dance. You see, that's really another style... (April 2008)

Something else that comes out of these observations is that the expression of such elective Africanity is sometimes combined with a social boundary: one that entails positioning oneself with respect to distinctive practices that leave a strong mark on the organization of nightlife in Veracruz. For example, during a collective discussion on the subject in one of the cafés at the Zócalo, a young artist who is a regular customer of the different landmark nightlife establishments in the historic centre of Veracruz describes this expression in his own way:

- I really prefer going there (Portal de Miranda) rather than to trendy (*Fresas*) discotheques on the Boulevard (coastal road). First, here the music is live, and it's free; you're in the street... You can come and go, have a beer, have a look at what's happening elsewhere, come back... Let's say it corresponds much better to my state of mind, the *Callejero* (street) spirit... That's the true spirit of Veracruz... isn't it? And most of all, what I can't stand in trendy places (*antros*) is the overly codified way you have to dress, walk, talk... look at others, while others make remarks about your clothes, the people you hang around with... Okay, they're not all like that; you have nicer places, more open you might say, but it's generally rather like that...
- And what's it like here?
- Well, in this kind of place, you do what you like; you don't have to ask yourself if you're okay or not; you can even enjoy doing the opposite, speaking bad, dressing wrong, doing all the things 'nice people' think is 'bad'.
- Meaning?
- Well, going to lower-class places, not being with a girl who spends all her time getting ready to go out... When Julia [his girlfriend] dresses *nice,*[11] - you see, with a dress, high heels, nail polish - I warn her: You're becoming *Fresa,*[12] and we laugh about it...
- And is it more a matter of listening to this kind of music with Afro-Caribbean influences than anything else?
- Well, this music recalls above all the past of the port (*Porteño*), slaves and pirates, contraband, all the night-life around the port, the wharves, the dockers, the popular cantinas around the market... and even I also like other musical genres and atmospheres, what I like most is the idea of being attracted to what 'decent folk' reject... (June 2008).

In other words, the issue here is sharing certain cultural practices with others to transform them into signs, signs that refer not only to 'popular' culture, but a way of life that strays somewhat from the norms set out by local 'polite society' (*gente bien*). In other words, signs of non-alignment with 'nice' people who go to certain trendy bars and 'speak with a lisp'[13] to emphasize their social distinction, or who have chosen to move away from the center of Veracruz to the cosier environment of the nearby municipality of Boca del Río, where the region's *Fresas* now gather in their clearly expressed will to emphasize social distance through greater spatial separation. And also signs that, by adopting the sexually explicit body movements of African dance and *Rumbera*, denote a common deviation from those who are also called 'decent people' (*gente decente*), one of whose characteristics involves precisely showing their moral distance from 'ordinary' folk[14] and rubbing out all that can appear as signs of Africanity in their way of displaying themselves to others.

Here, the display of physical traits, postures, gestures and aesthetics referring to the different cultural styles evoking the African heritage is a way of expressing one's empathy with *Callejera* (street) culture that develops its own reinterpretation of ethnic boundaries and maintains an elective relationship with Africa and the black Americas. And it is also a way of positioning oneself in a class through signs attributed locally to the different 'origins' of *mestizaje*. Like 'speaking with a lisp' or dancing 'like a Black' are social markers based on a shared belief in the common origins forming local society. This belief can be more or less well accepted or rejected, and the cultural and physical traits associated with it more or less displayed or concealed, blackened or whitened. It is indeed in this way that expressions of 'Black identity' observable in such contexts are not *despite*, but rather *because of* a representation of *mestizaje* that entails constant reference to one or the other of these different 'roots' that leads individuals to position themselves socially, physically and culturally with respect to supposed 'African roots'.

Conclusion

The approach to this research, of which some empirical elements have been presented here, seeks to portray a broader perspective than those focusing solely on the political embryos that strive towards collective mobilization of 'Black identity' awareness which is associated with the experience of domination and discrimination. The analysis focuses on the processes whereby ethnic definitions referring to the 'African roots' of *mestizaje*, phenotypic traits more or less perceived as 'Black' and 'Black' or 'African' cultural characteristics are carried, interpreted or circumvented by different types of social actors in more or less stable, durable or variable ways according to context and situation. Since Fredrik Barth's seminal text (Barth 1969), the processes of creation-transformation of boundaries and the activities of agents and agencies striving for their recognition and social legitimacy or, conversely, their disappearance, have been the subject of many studies and theoretical analyses. Recently, Andreas Wimmer listed the different contributions to a comparative approach focusing on a 'boundary-making approach' in ethnicity studies and proposed a new taxonomy that attempts to organize conceptually the ways in which social actors participate in the transformations of ethnic boundaries (Wimmer 2008a, b). However, this overinvestment in historical and political processes aiming to stabilize or obscure the social meaning of such boundaries does not account for situations where boundaries take on meaning for the social actors and contribute to social life. From this standpoint, the focus on scenes from urban life, definitions of cultural policy or rationales of social distinction suggests research orientations to help better understand: the ambiguity of such boundaries, various interpretations of social scenes, ethnic categorizations that function only in certain areas of social life all while contributing to its organization, vague stereotypes that are sometimes mobilized in courses of action, and plays on appearances.

On the basis of Bastide's dialectical approach, it is possible to account for the processes observed by analyzing them in terms of 'stable instability' and 'unstable stability'.[15] The former can be taken to mean the relative permanence of the fluidity of ethnic boundaries. In public policy concerning 'African roots', as in touristic descriptions of Veracruz or in the ordinary situations of social life, nothing can support the idea that this fluidity is threatened by rationales for radicalizing differences or toughening identities. As we have seen, here ethnic boundaries find meaning in their relationships with representations of *mes-*

tizaje and its 'roots'. They are not merely 'surviving' the reality of *mestizaje* until they disappear; quite the contrary, they are constantly fuelled by a representation of *mestizaje* recalling the 'heritages', 'peoples' and 'races' composing it.

At the same time, the 'stable instability' of ethnic boundaries is accompanied by 'unstable stability'. It is by moving from negation of the African heritage and the undertaking to whiten the stereotyped frames of *Jarocha* identity to recognition of the African roots in *mestizaje* that most of the phenomena observed in this study take on their meaning. And if they have found a certain historical permanence, nothing suggests that this will persist. Transnational trends towards the formation of collective awareness of belonging to the same group, supported by international development agencies, may get the better of this specific relationship observed in the city of Veracruz between the representations of *mestizaje* and enacted ethnicity.

Notes

1. Translated by ATTIC Traduction Interprétariat, Nice. Revision by Laura Schuft (URMIS, Nice).

2. Some authors have recently begun showing interest in this (Malcomson, 2010; Moreno Figueroa, 2006; Sue, 2007).

3. In particular, it is part of research conducted from 2002 to 2006 in the context of the IDYMOV program, *Identidades y movilidades, las sociedades regionales frente a los nuevos contextos políticos y migratorios. Una comparación entre México y Colombia* (IRD-CIESAS-ICANH).

4. In Brubaker's terms, unlike 'groupism', the tendency to consider ethnic groups, nations and races as substantial entities, the notion of 'groupness' refers to an event, something that may occur - or not - in the social world, may be crystallized - or not - despite identity entrepreneurs' efforts to impose their existence (Brubaker 2002).

5. See, for example, García Díaz, 2002; Pasquel, 1979; Pérez Montfort, 2001.

6. See *Historia del Hotel Mocambo*, information leaflet distributed by Hotel Mocambo Veracruz.

7.   http://www.travelbymexico.com/veracruz (consulted on 26 November 2009).

8.   The name given to this *Son* of Cuban origin to distinguish it from *Son Jarocho*. The different episodes since its arrival in the 1920s and its adoption in Veracruz with the formation of bands are recounted by many analysts of local cultural life (Figueroa Hernández 2002, García Díaz 2002a, González 2007, Mac Masters 1995).

9.   Literally, 'Veracruz is the Caribbean, too'.

10. In Cuba, the word *guarachero* refers to a musician who composes and sings *la guaracha*, a satirical musical genre, viewed as a playful person who falls in love easily.

11. English word used locally to refer to others or oneself as *la gente nice* (nice people) featured in celebrity magazines or, more modestly, in the VIP pages of regional daily newspapers.

12. 'Well-born young people' or, more derogatorily, 'rich kid' ['mama's boy'] in the local taxonomy.

13. The Spanish expression *'hablar con la zeta'* is used locally to refer to Spaniards who pronounce the letters 'c' and 'z' with a lisp like the English 'th', unlike most Mexicans, except to evoke one's Spanish origins with some snobbery.

14. Such expressions as *gente fea, gente corriente, gente vulgar, gente coloniera* are all used in the local taxonomy to refer to people who are poor, unrefined and vulgar from the working-class districts of Veracruz.

15. Roger Bastide borrowed the terms *continuous discontinuity* and *discontinuous continuity* from Georges Gurvitch to attempt to exceed the opposition structuring the field of Black studies in the Americas around analyses in terms of continuity, dear to Melville Herskovits, or discontinuity, according to Franklin Frazier (Bastide 1996).

Bibliography

Anonymous. 1940. *Veracruz, México*. Veracruz: Asociación Mexicana de Turismo - Departamento de Turismo de la Secretaría de Gobernación.

Barth, Fredrik. 1969. Introduction. *Ethnic Groups and Boundaries*, ed. F. Barth. Oslo: University Press.

Bastide, Roger. 1996. Continuité et discontinuité des sociétés et des cultures afro-américaines. *Bastidiana (Les Amériques noires et la recherche afro-américaniste)* 13-14: 77-88.

Bonfil Batalla, Guillermo. 1990. *México profundo. Una civilización negada.* México: CNCA-Grijalbo.

Brubaker, Rogers. 2002. Ethnicity without Groups. *Archives Européennes de Sociologie* XLIII (2): 163-189.

Bullock, William. 1992. Seis meses de residencia y viajes en México. In *Cien viajeros en Veracruz. Crónicas y relatos* III, 1822-1830, ed. M. Poblett Miranda. México: Gobierno del Estado de Veracruz.

Cruz Carretero, Sagrario, 2005. Yanga and the Black Origins of Mexico. *The Review of Black Political Economy* 33 (1). Special symposium: The Black Presence in Mexico, September.

Delgado Calderón, Alfredo. 2004. *Historia, cultura e identidad en el Sotavento.* México: Conaculta.

Flores Martos, Juan Antonio. 2004. *Portales de múcara. Una etnografía del puerto de Veracruz.* Xalapa (Veracruz): Universidad Veracruzana.

García de León, Antonio. 1992. El Caribe afroandaluz: permanencia de una civilización popular. *La Jornada Semanal* 135: 27-33, 12 de Enero.

García de León, Antonio. 1992. Con la vida en un danzón: notas sobre el movimiento inquilinario de Veracruz en 1922. In *Actores sociales en un proceso de transformación: Veracruz en los años veinte*, ed. M. Reyna Muñoz. Xalapa, Ver: Universidad Veracruzana, 33-53.

García Díaz, Bernardo. 1998. El Veracruz de Joaquín Santamaría. In *Joaquín Santamaría, Sol de plata*, ed. A. Tovalín Ahumada. México: Universidad Veracruzana, 24-60.

García Díaz, Bernardo. 2002. Veracruz en la primera mitad del siglo XIX. Testimonios de viajeros. In *La Habana/Veracruz Veracruz/La Habana. Las dos orillas*, eds B. García Díaz y S. Guerra Vilaboy. Veracruz: Universidad Veracruzana, Universidad de la Habana, 215-238.

Guadarrama Olivera, Horacio. 2002. Los carnavales del puerto de Veracruz. In *La Habana/Veracruz, Veracruz/La Habana Las dos orillas*, eds B Garcia Diaz y S. Guerra Vilaboy. México: Universidad Veracruziana/Universidad de la Habana, 469-493.

Jiménez Illescas Gloria ed. 2002. *La ruta del son. Guía touristica Región Costera del Sotavento del Estado de Veracruz*. Xalapa: Gobierno del Estado de Veracruz.

Jiménez, Lucina. 2006. *Políticas culturales en transición. Retos y escenarios de la gestión cultural en México*. México: Conaculta .

Lara Millán, Gloria. 2008. *Política, espacio y construcción social del poder local-regional en la Costa Chica de Oaxaca*. Tesis de doctorado en Antropología, Centro de Investigación y Estudios Superiores en Antropología Social (CIESAS), México.

Lewis, Laura A. 2000. Blacks, Black Indians, Afromexicans: The Dynamics of Race, Nation, and Identity in a Mexican 'moreno' Community (Guerrero). *American Ethnologist* 27 (4): 898-926.

Malcomson, Hettie. 2010. *Creative Standardization: Danzon and the Port of Veracruz, Mexico*. PhD Thesis, Department of Sociology (PPSIS). Cambridge: University of Cambridge, Department of Anthropology.

Moreno Figueroa, Mónica. 2006. *The Complexities of the Visible: Mexican Women's Experiences of Racism, Mestizaje and National Identity*. Londres: Goldsmiths College, University of London.

Pasquel, Leonardo. 1979. *Viajeros en el Estado de Veracruz*. México: Citlaltépetl, Colección Suma Veracruzana, Serie Viajeros.

Pérez Montfort, Ricardo. 2001. El jarocho y sus fandangos vistos por viajeros y cronistas extranjeros de los siglos XIX y XX. Apuntas para la historia de la formación de un estereotipo regional. In *Veracruz y sus viajeros*. México: Gobierno del Estado de Veracruz, 123-187.

Pérez Montfort, Ricardo. 2003. *Estampas de nacionalismo popular mexicano. Diez ensayos sobre cultura popular y nacionalismo*. México: CIESAS.

Pérez Montfort, Ricardo. 2007. El 'negro' y la negritud en la formación del estereotipo del jarocho durante los siglos XIX y XX. In *Expresiones populares y estereotipos culturales en México. Siglos XIX y XX. Diez ensayos*. México: CIESAS, 175-210.

Poblett Miranda, Martha ed. 1992. *Cien viajeros en Veracruz. Crónicas y relatos*. México: Gobierno del Estado de Veracruz, 11 tomos.

Raymond, Nathalie. 2004. Las interrogantes que platea América Latina al estudio del fenómeno turístico. *Trace* (45) 11-31.

Sue, Christina Alicia. 2007. *Race and national ideology in Mexico: an ethnographic study of racism, color, mestizaje and blackness in Veracruz.* PhD thesis of Sociology. Los Angeles: UCLA.

Sue, Christina Alicia. 2009. The Dynamics of Color: Mestizaje, Racism and Blackness in Veracruz, Mexico. In *Shades of difference: why skin color matters,* ed. E. N. Glenn. Stanford Calif.: Stanford University Press, 114-128.

Wimmer, Andreas. 2008a. Elementary of ethnic boundary making. *Ethnic and Racial Studies* 31, (6): 1025-1055.

Wimmer, Andreas. 2008b. The Making and Unmaking of Ethnic Boundaries: A Multilevel Process Theory. *American Journal of Sociology* 113 (4): 970-1022.

Chapter 7

Transnational networks and re-Africanization of the *Santería* in Mexico City[1]

Nahayeilli B. Juárez Huet

Today, Mexico is an important country in the reception and dissemination of Cuban *Santería*.[2] In Mexico City and its metropolitan zone, the number of initiates, consultants,[3] and people, who in some way or another appropriate one or more aspects of *Santería* relative to its deities, music, ritual paraphernalia has increased notably since the 1990's. In contrast to earlier decades, the media and channels for its diffusion have not only multiplied but also diversified and in consequence, the number of cities within Mexico where its presence can be observed has also grown, especially over the last fifteen years[4] (Guadalajara, Monterrey, Morelos, Acapulco, Morelia, Mérida, Cancún, Campeche, Villahermosa, Veracruz).

Although it should also be pointed out that it is difficult to talk in terms of numbers, *Santería* is still a minority religion with respect to dominant Catholicism and as it is not recognized as a Religious Association there is no official record of affiliates. Needless to say the census is still unable to account for the complexity and diversity of the religious practices and beliefs observed in Mexico. Despite this, not only Mexicans but also foreign initiates (Cubans, Nigerians, Americans, Venezuelans, Puerto Ricans...) recognize the growth potential of the *Orisha* religion in Mexico.

The presence and growth of *Santería* in Mexico can be understood and analyzed as a transnational religious process that is related to the cultural, political and economic spheres (Glick-Schiller and Fouron 1999). This process has been helped by cultural industries, communication technologies and the physical mobility (migration and tourism) of many of its adepts and believers situated in a diverse number of locations around the world (mainly in Americas, Europe and Africa). The flow of ideas, practices, discourses and objects conveyed along these channels enables the exchanges and mutual influences through the transnational networks (religious, artistic, political, commercial ...) that are recreated within specific contexts. Thus, the locations and individuals interconnected by these networks can be seen as part of "a single field of social relationships," that is to say, a transnational social field (Basch, Glick-Schiller and Blanc Szanton 1994). This approach gives us a better understanding of the specific nature of the processes of trans-nationalization and relocation of *Santería* in Mexico, by considering them as part of broader ones. By relocation I mean the process through which *Santería* and/or its symbols and paraphernalia are adapted and sometimes transformed *ad hoc* along with the socio-cultural features of the "new" contexts in which they circulate. These forms of appropriation are expressed most clearly in the field of religious praxis.

In contrast to Cuba, the original socio-cultural and geographic context of *Santería*, where it has achieved recognition as an emblem of African culture and heritage forming part of the Cuban nation and culture, or in the United States where it was adopted by Afro-Americans as part of their ancestral heritage, in the case of Mexico City and also in other cities in the interior, this religion does not claim to have any ethnic links to the "Afro-Mexican" population. Like other symbols of Afro-American culture, *Santería* circulates and expands without necessarily linking itself to ethnic issues. In other words, *Santería* in Mexico does not link itself to African heritage, even though recently the music, dance and rituals of *Santería* have been part of the official programs in cultural festivals that have exalted the African legacy in Mexico and Latin America.

In recent years, there has been a movement – still incipient – that aims to "revive" the African Yoruba tradition that *Santería* forms part of. This movement exists within a broader and more dynamic one on a transnational scale that is developing with political and ideological intersections that go beyond the frontiers of the "strictly" religious. In this paper I will present a case study of México City and its metropolitan zone, this being the place where the seeds of the movement were sown in Mexico.

Brief overview: Trans-nationalization and relocation of *Santería* in Mexico

I. The first stage of the trans-nationalization of *Santería*[5] in Mexico can be situated towards the end of the 1940s and the beginning of the 1950s and is closely linked to the music, cinema, and show business industries. During this period, the spread of *Santería*, or rather, of some of its elements, especially music and dance, due to the mediation of these industries, were often de-contextualized, desecrated, and deformed. In this way, these industries converted the world of *Santería* not only into something exotic and even erotic, but also something barbarian and savage. *Santería* involved "blacks" and mulattos belonging to a world historically constructed as marginal and primitive. It was practiced by a number of Cuban artists who immigrated to Mexico during that period, some of whom had grown up in neighborhoods of Havana that were known for their "Afro-Cuban religious tradition." The only way of gaining access to this world was through the Cuban connection. Independently of their veracity, it is not accidental that references were made by Mexican *santeros* regarding Mexican artistes of the time supposedly initiated into *Santería*, and who shared credits on the big screen with Cuban musicians and dancers who were initiated in this religion. It should be pointed out however, that the physical mobility of visitors to both countries was not confined to the artistic field. So it is possible to identify some Mexicans who, on a trip to Cuba received *resguardos*,[6] minor degrees of initiation, or requested "spiritual works" from *santeros* (Juárez Huet 2004). In fact these were very incipient cases – compared to what we can observe today – as *Santería* was not accessible to outsiders and even less to foreigners. At the same time, we should take into account that up to this time, Afro-Cuban cults were considered as "witchcraft" in Cuba itself and were associated with "intellectual primitivism," vestiges of the African heritage. An example of this is to be found in the early work of Fernando Ortiz, the father of Afro-Cuban studies, who was influenced by the Positivism and Social Evolutionism of the period and analyzed these forms of religious expression from a criminological perspective (Menéndez, 2002; Hagedorn, 2001:174). Ortiz believed that the "black race" was harmful for Cuban society because of "its superstitions, its organizations, its languages, its dances." (Ortiz 2001, 5)

Thus, at the beginning of the twentieth century "all trace of Africanism, particularly with reference to magical-religious practices, was mercilessly opposed." (Argyriadis 2000, 651) Although since colonial times the various campaigns against these supposed "atavisms" led, for example, to legislation to abolish all Afro-Cuban musical activity (Moore, ibid.: 178). In later years the African heritage was "legitimized and revalued" as part of the miscegenation *(mestizaje)* of the Cuban nation and culture, thanks to the Afro-Cuban movement of the 1920s and the influence of European intellectuals and artists who made "negro" and "primitive" art fashionable (Brandon 1999, Menéndez 2002, Agyriadis 2006).

It should be pointed out that, despite the legitimacy that some Afro-Cuban religions achieved due to the artists and intellectuals of this movement, this was in fact relative as they were treated with an ambiguity that "continued to oscillate between periods of relative tolerance and periods of repression (…)" (Brandon 1993, 94) as aesthetic valuation was not the same as legitimizing religious practices "judged criminal and violent." (Argyriadis 2006, 48) On the same subject, Martínez Furé notes that during the republican period the prejudices inherited from colonial times led the government to "stamp on everything that

denoted the African presence in Cuba" and one of the informants he cites relates how "when one was least expecting it, the
police appeared and took the *soperas* [term applied generically
to all *orisha* vessels] with the saints, the necklaces and even
slashed the skins on the drums in front of us." (1979, 185-186)

II. We have to wait for the waves of Cuban migrants to the
United States after Castro came to power to observe the first
changes in the spread of *Santería* in Mexico. Up until this period,
the possibilities of gaining access to this religious world were
mainly geographically confined to Cuba where, despite being
recognized as part of the national culture and popular folklore,
Afro-Cuban cults continued to be practiced "clandestinely" as
they were considered – as were all religions – the "opium of the
people." (Brandon 1993, 101, Argyriadis 1999, 51, Knauer 2001)

With the Cuban migration to the United States and the
consequent spread of *Santería* to a number of American cities
(Brandon 1993), in the long run different options became available, other than Cuba, for Mexicans to be initiated into *Santería*.
In this respect, it is important to stress that Miami, where two
thirds of the Cuban population in the United States was concentrated during this period (Argyriadis and Capone 2004), was
the American city where Mexicans and even Cubans resident in
Mexico City tended to prefer for initiation. The Cuban *santeros*,
who came to Mexico City either before or after immigrating
to the United States, established ritual kinship[7] with Mexicans
who contributed to the spreading of *Santería* in that city. By the
second half of the 1970s, Mexico City and some nearby urban
zones also began to be options for carrying out initiation ceremonies.

In this way, the trans-nationalization of *Santería* in Mexico
– now also as a religious option – has become interwoven with
the process of trans-nationalization with other contexts such
as the United States. It should also be noted that the Mexicans
initiated during those decades did not dedicate themselves to
the religion, nor were they prolific godparents, in contrast to
the Cubans *santeros*, whose ritual authority was also not questioned. It was a religion that was kept largely hidden, although

to the contrary of Cuba, it was not clandestine and its Mexican initiates belonged to the middle and middle-high strata. It was not until the end of the 1980s when the Matamoros "narco-satánicos" scandal (1989)[8] showed how, during this decade, *Santería* initiates and consultants were not only on the increase but also that the social strata involved were diversifying and that their ritual kinship networks extended to Cuba, the United States, and Mexico. This also brought *Santería* into public view and associated ambiguously – above all in the press – with drug trafficking, delinquency, and Satanism (Juárez Huet 2004, 2007).

III. The 1990s mark another important change in this process.[9] The growth in the number of practitioners and believers in Mexico has encouraged greater competition amongst the followers. This situation is also helped by the Cuban context in which the "Afro-Cuban" culture, including the whole universe of its religious expressions – in particular *Santería* and its Yoruba elements – has been one of the areas that has received most impetus in Cuba's tourist industry (Hagedorn 2001, 8, 221, Knauer 2001, 23). I should add that Cuba's difficult economic situation has led the population to generate survival strategies linked to the field of tourism and religious "mercantilism." (Argyriadis 2005) In Mexico City it can commonly be observed that earnings obtained as *derecho* (material/spiritual recompense) generated by ritual services such as consultations, "cleansings", and initiations, have become the main or complementary means of subsistence for the initiated. This situation of competition generates conflicts and mutual accusations of "spiritually illicit" profit. It is always the "other priest who "commercializes the religion" and who "makes a living from the saint rather than living for the saint."

On the other hand, the plasticity characteristic of *Santería* is more evident. In fact, its original complementary nature interweaves and is reinforced within two cultural frameworks that in Mexico function as factors that drive its dissemination and also its often complementary appropriation in religious praxis. On one hand, with the traditions of pre-Hispanic and colonial roots linked to the practices of popular Catholicism and also

Marian Trinitarian Spiritualism, and on the other, with the neo-esoteric practices that have become equally visible in the past fifteen years. This phenomenon has led to *santeros* and tradespeople of a lot of the paraphernalia of *Santería*, take advantage of a variety of environments and channels through which the objects and services of *Santería* are advertised, commercialized, and offered in the same way as those of other "traditions."

These environments also encourage direct forms of relocation as *Santería* and many of its elements frequently circulate, re-semanticized, and transformed into merchandise that often forms only a part of what Gutiérrez Zúñiga defines as "exoteric store shelving." (Gutiérrez Zúñiga 2007, 367) The image of *Santería* and some of its elements circulate as "protectors," "propitiators" (of "good" or "evil"), means of "divining" or linked to "questions of magic" or of "witchcraft," without this necessarily implying further involvement than this, that is, religious initiation. This phenomenon has also generated a division between members of the religion, as many disqualify and speak out against the dissemination, "trivialization," and "commercializing" of the religion's "secrets."

On the other hand, it should be mentioned that despite its growth, *Santería* is not recognized as a religion in Mexico, frequently being categorized as a "sect" and is still quite stigmatized. However, this is not limited to Mexico. As Frigerio has emphasized, once they shift to other contexts the different Afro-American religions need to reacquire the social position that they had achieved in the places of origin where, with only a few exceptions, they are considered "true religions." (Frigerio 2004, 24).

Yoruba "rules"

In recent years, Mexicans have become increasingly interested in the "back to the roots" movement or what some researchers call the "re-Africanization" movement (Capone 1999, Frigerio 2004) that exalts the Yoruba culture and legacy and aims to "desyncretize" and "purge" the Afro-American religions of foreign elements (such as Christian ones, for example). Encouraged by a Nigerian elite, this movement elected as its flag

171

a universalist religion (which originates from Ile Ife, Nigeria) "with access for anyone, regardless of their ethnic origin or nationality, and whose Mecca and model to follow is: the Yorubaland." (Frigerio 2004)

A number of authors have stressed the transnationality that has characterized the Afro-American religions since the nineteenth century (Matory 1998, 2000, Peel 2000, Frigerio 2004, Capone 2000, 2004) that, as Matory underlines, were thought for a long time to be "survivals" of an ancestral African past, when "(...) in fact they form part of a quite modern and multinational movement of political and literary inspiration (...) a movement that could be called 'Yoruba Revival.'" (1998:44) The same author places the background of this movement in the Lagosian Renaissance of the late nineteenth century and from which, of all the religions of African origin that were implanted in America, it was the Yoruba that achieved a leading role and a greater degree of international prestige. The key actors in the cultural nationalism that emerge in Lagos, thanks to which certain merit was afforded to traditional religion (Peel 2000 279), held traditional Yoruba culture up "as proof of dignity of the black race." (Matory 1998, 176) The interest in studying and describing it was not only a subject for the devotees but also of intellectuals of the period (anthropologists, historians, missionaries, writers, and literary and art critics) (Matory 1998, 264) who contributed to the dissemination of this superiority in the   New World (for Brazil see Capone 2000, for Cuba see Argyriadis 2000).

The national context as an arena for conflicts between coreligionists

In Mexico the tendency to consider Cuba as the legitimate source of *Santería* still predominates and this has meant that nationality is still held up as a symbolic resource in the dynamics of often conflictive relations between practitioners. It is common for Mexican *santeros* or *babalawos*[10] to consider that being initiated in Cuba or having a Cuban godfather is a "ritual guarantee," that is to say, that their initiation ceremonies were done according to the "tradition of origin," Cuban.

Mexico City (and its conurbation) can be considered a node that is connected – by means of national and transnational networks – in positions of complementation, competition, and subordination with respect to other nodes within the transnational field of which it forms a part. On a national level, Mexico City concentrates the largest number of *Santería* initiates and has enough prime materials and human resources for the different festivities and initiation ceremonies. Most of Mexico's oldest *santeros* (both Mexican and Cuban) live there. It is also established as the principal location for the production and distribution of paraphernalia of *Santería* in the whole country. It is a place of dense traffic and the confluence of a great diversity of networks and flows linked to the *Orisha* religion, but on the transnational scale with respect to Cuba, its national "strategic position" becomes relative. While Cuba symbolically enjoys the prestige afforded by being *Santería*'s place of origin and the bearer of this religious tradition, Mexico has not yet achieved the status that will permit it a position of competition but rather one of subordination.

As Mexico is still not considered a legitimate bearer of the Yoruba religious "tradition," neither, except perhaps in a few cases, are Mexican priests, although there are those who defend their position, especially those who have been initiated into this religion for many years. However, the lack of familiarity of this practice and the less abundant offer of religious specialists in comparison with Cuba make the Mexican scene a favorable location for Cuban *santeros* or *babalawos*, as they have the advantage of being able to position themselves "right away" in a more prestigious status with respect to Mexicans, when in Cuba they are perhaps just "one of many."

It is in this context that amongst *santeros* there is always someone who says that the Cubans are "over-bearing;" that "they feel like they are the kings of Mexico;" that given the economic conditions on the island, when they come to Mexico "they go wild" or "take advantage of the unwary." They are also "accused" of "making money out of religion"[11] and even of "disliking Mexico." One of my informants who has been involved in *Santería* for more than ten years and is quite "disillusioned with the Cubans" comments on this subject:

"I feel better amongst Mexicans (in the religious setting) because we think differently from them (the Cubans), I think that because our people were not enslaved, were they? Nor do we have a Fidel and their system has made them as they are, in other words they come here to turn themselves into Fidels, to do everything they can't do in their own country, because they don't like Mexico, the food is bad, the women are ugly, the best is in Cuba".[12]

The grievance of the Mexicans towards some of their Cuban coreligionists also has to do with their perception that "they give them little importance," "they look down on them," or that "they don't give them fair credit," even when they reach a higher position or "age" in religious terms, that means years of initiation – a fundamental criterion in the dynamics of the power relations amongst the religious followers. Another equally common reproach towards the Cubans is their lack of generosity with respect to their ritual knowledge. In theory this is transmitted from the elders to the younger members (that is, from godparents to godchildren). However, this has not diminished the Mexicans' interest in making initiations in Cuba, nor in the proliferation and operation of transnational networks of ritual kinship, and ritual collaboration between priests of both nationalities. In fact, relations are strongly subjected to contextual circumstances, and although power relations based on "race" are not evident, it does not mean that they are completely absent.

At the same time, in some cases skin color can come into play as symbolic capital. Mexicans are often pointed to by their fellow countrymen as *"malinchistas"* to explain their preference for "outsiders." And in the case of *Santería*, both Mexicans and Cubans have told me that when the *santeros* or *babalawos* as well as being Cuban, are black or mulatto, the impression they often have on some Mexicans (especially consultants) is that this makes them "more effective," in that they are "more authentic." That is to say there is in México an underlying association between this religion and being black. So, it could be said that in some way black priests are regarded as beings who possess "special and particularly magic powers (… and) they preserved a certain fascination" (Wade 1997, 55) since the colonial period. A fascination that in some cities like Mexico City or Guadalajara for example, also expresses a vision of the black, tinged in a certain way with "exoticism" and "foreignness."

While *Santería*'s African heritage is familiar to the practitioners in Mexico, until now no attempt has been made to claim it as a form of cultural heritage, a product of the presence of black and "Afro-Mexican" populations.[13] This distinctive characteristic which, as I have mentioned, contrasts with the case of Cuba or of the United States, can perhaps be explained by the fact that in the discourse of the "Mexican nation" emphasis has been placed on it being the product of the "mestizaje" or racial mix of the Indian and Spaniard (Martínez Montiel 1995, Lomnitz 1995). The population of African origin is not recognized as part of this, lacks an "external characterization on the part of the State." and is also "politically non-existent." (Hoffman 2006, 107, 124)

Very few of my informants know that there were slave populations of African origin in almost all the regions of Mexico nor that there still exists a number of "Afro-Mexican" communities (Aguirre Beltrán 1989, Montiel 1995). Those that are even aware of this phenomenon commonly "distance themselves" from this root, meaning that they do not identify the possibility of their coming from it, and contrast themselves from people with dark skin, "frizzy (tightly curled) hair, flat nose and thick lips," supposedly characteristics of people from regions with population of African origin on the Gulf or the Pacific coast of Mexico. Sometimes they also reproduce the "integration thesis" (Hoffman 2006) of the academic environment, which states that the African who arrived here ended up being "diluted" or "assimilated in the "*mestizaje*" or – to quote one informant – in "the Mexican genetic composition." This is illustrated, for example, by the case of a Mexican *babalawo* who had "recently" learnt about the black presence in Mexico.[14] In an academic forum held in Havana, where he participated as a speaker, he said,

> "The first thing to attract our attention when we see a black or mulatto walking around the streets of Mexico City or Guadalajara, is their strangeness, as

it is hard to find an Afro-American in our cities. We ask ourselves, "Are they Cuban?" If we approach this individual and we make inquiries, I assure you that in 99% of the cases, they are foreigners". As an example of this, Don Pedro Montero, a mechanic from the black village of Cuajinicuilapa, (precisely the place in which Aguirre Beltrán did his first ethnography on this subject), told a Reuters reporter: "In Mexico City people think I am foreign and try to speak to me in English, and they look at me incredulously when I speak to them in Spanish and tell them that I am a black from the Costa Chica in Mexico."

He added immediately afterwards that in his presentation he would try to explain to those present that, "the process of *mestizaje* (...) absorbed the black race, its customs, its beliefs, its art, until it almost completely disappeared in my Mexico. I had to import a pretty *mulatica*,[15] who I adore, to have a string of the African race in my house in Guadalajara."[16] Thus, in this context, it would be difficult for a movement aimed at vindicating and appropriating *Santería* as an "Afro-Mexican" cultural legacy to germinate.

Networks and nodes: "the go-between"

As a consequence of the impact of transnational networks with Nigerians, the positions of greatest prestige that were once occupied mainly by Cubans, are now being counteracted by the Re-Africanization movement that raises Africa (western Africa, particularly Nigeria) and not Cuba as the legitimate source of the religion. In Mexico, it is also a process that pursues a greater degree of independence from the original religious mentors, in this case Cuban "guardianship," as Frigerio rightly points out for other contexts (Frigerio 2004, 52).

In the eyes of Mexican leaders involved in the movement, it is necessary to "retrieve" part of the "original" African tradition that over the years was "lost" in Cuba. In this way, more Mexicans are beginning to be interested in making contact with and getting initiated by Nigerians and/or priests of other nationalities who have been initiated by them. They take Yoruba classes (to better understand the ritual language) and collect specialized literature on the subject (written by anthropologists, academics, and foreign practitioners). They also organize activities (lectures, workshops, courses, etc.) in which they involve "traditionalist" priests in order to start "correcting" the path of their religious practice. This "intellectualization" through access to specialized literature and the incorporation of a number of elements brought from contemporary Africa into present day religious practice, is what Prandi calls to "Africanize" (1998, 162), or what other authors call to "Re-Africanize." (Capone 1999, Frigerio 2004)

Today, this phenomenon is a characteristic aspect of the transnational social field, in which both "the tradition" of the American religious diaspora and that of Africa, despite recognizing that they are united, oppose each other in their different "models of tradition." (Capone 1999) Those involved in this movement defend the name "Yoruba religion," "*Orisha* religion," or "*Orisha* tradition" as the "correct" one. They often disqualify "syncretism" and try to purge their religious praxis of Christian elements that over time were incorporated in Latin America contexts. In Mexico, some Cubans also consider themselves part of the re-Africanization movement. However, although they recognize Africa as the "essential matrix" of (the wrongly called) *Santería*, Cuba remains the legitimate original point of reference for their form of religious praxis or "model of tradition." While this religion may have suffered "deviations" and could possibly be "enriched," it does not mean that it should be disposed, especially since "it has been the Cubans that made this religion known in America."

The transnational networks established by the so-called "traditionalists" of the "Yoruba religion" have nourished and reconfigured the power relations in the Mexican context. One of the most obvious effects – and which years ago was already visible in other countries where *Santería*'s presence was felt – can be seen in the growing interest in "formalizing" sub-networks to achieve a legitimacy that could be played out in various ways at a local, national, or transnational scale. Certain node leaders and actors – those that maintain a dense multiplexity and key positioning within the sub-networks to which they belong – are pushing for associative and organizational forms aimed at setting up more "institutionalized" religious networks. What in theory gives them cohesion are the interests that are perceived, or at least held up to be shared or necessary to achieve determined objectives (social legitimacy, inter-group legitimacy, recognition of the "Yoruba religion" as universal, religious unification, legal recognition, etc.) offering an organizational base for their expression. Affiliation is not based on the criteria of ritual kinship but rather on the "acceptance" or identification with a (supposed) common project that is not however appropriated equally, as I will try to illustrate in the cases of the *Ilé Ifá* Association of México and the Mexican chapter of HATTAF (International).

Ilé Ifá Association of Mexico

The *Ilé Ifá* Association of Mexico, founded in 2003, is led by the Cuban Leonel Gámez, recognized as one of the most prestigious *babalawos* in Mexico City where he has lived since 1991. His interest in creating a legally constituted association emerged on account of his contact with a number of Nigerian leaders at the head of the International Congress of Orisa Tradition and Culture (Orisa Congress) for which he was appointed representative in Mexico at the end of the 1990s. These conferences have become "privileged places for the elaboration of the 'African (Yoruba) tradition'" (Capone 2005) and transformed into the arena for the conflicts around legitimacy and authority on ritual and philosophical knowledge of Yoruba culture and religion.[17] The initiatives aimed at the unity and orthodoxy within the cults in which the "Yoruba identity" has become the common denominator, are faced with what its president, Nigerian Wande Abímbola, calls a "fragmented world."

Gámez, who is light-skinned, later gave up this appointment due to his disagreement on "the racism shown by some Afro-Americans (from the United States) about accepting whites in the religion," but above all because some Nigerians, according to him, "want to impose their criteria (...) to push aside and minimize the Cubans." In this sense, the interest in what he calls "traditionalism" in Nigeria is not the same as "stamping out" the tradition of the (Cuban) Diaspora or aimed at re-initiating himself "in the African way" as some have done. This would mean denying and negating the validity and legitimacy of religious practice in Cuba thanks to which "this religion became known" in America. However, this does not invalidate his interest in learning the language, prayers, and songs in the Yoruba language that with time were "degraded" in America. Gámez starts out from the idea that the variations of the Afro-American religions in each country are the product of the distance of the slaves from the land of their birth for which reason, "they gradually got a little distorted from the original, [that is to say] from the original religion of the Yoruba." For this *babalawo* "traditionalism" implies revitalizing the African roots and with this, purging the Yoruba religion of any Catholic influence.

In keeping with this position, he founded his association with the aim of "promoting and encouraging knowledge of the culture and traditions of the Yoruba religion in Mexico." This implies "unifying" criteria with respect to ritual practice, looking for points of agreement that permit "unification." However, the main obstacle he faces in order to achieve this goal, is precisely the degree of variation that exists in the religious practice of the different religious kinship lineages. This is the main reason for his strategy of slow and gradual religious "unification." Gámez believes that it is only through the teaching of prayers, the history of the deities and the concepts of religion within the Yoruba culture that the religious praxis in Latin America will eventually "recover" what has been "lost." *Ilé Ifá* is an association that puts its faith in religious "traditionalism" in order to achieve broader social and legal recognition to counteract stigmatization.

HATTAF Mexico

This interest in providing certified and formal "instruction for priests" is also one of the objectives of the International African Temple of Healing and Teaching, a branch in Mexico of HATTAF *International*.[18] It was founded in Lagos, Nigeria in 1988 by the Nigerian Chief *Ifagbenusola* Atanda, current treasurer of the International Congress of Orisa Tradition and Culture. The branch temples of HATTAH International are located in Africa, Europe, and the Americas.[19] The birth of this temple in Mexico, in March 2004, was achieved thanks to the alliance between Chief *Ifagbenusola* Atanda and the then Mexican *oriaté*[20] Eli Torres who, in 2003, was named Delegate for Mexico at the Eighth International Congress of Orisa Tradition and Culture held in Havana. Torres, whose relations with some of his Cuban coreligionists in Mexico, especially with Gámez, have not always been cordial, figures as one of the major Mexican "activists" in the incipient re-Africanization movement in this country. Years before, he had already been in contact with other "traditionalist" initiates in the religion resident in Spain and the United States, some of whom had visited Mexico. He organized workshops on Yoruba religion with Falokun Fatumbí, a North American *babalawo* initiated in Nigeria. After his attendance and appointment at the Eighth Orisa Congress, he managed to bring Wande Abímbola, leader and founder of the International Orisa Congress, to Mexico to give a lecture on Yoruba religion and to provide with "traditionalist" initiations to devotees in Mexico just as they are practiced in Yorubaland. Torres also became the president of HATTAF Mexico for a few months.

Membership of HATTAF offers to its mainly Mexican associates the opportunity of initiation in Nigeria[21] as well as a certification for all those who pass the corresponding exams for initiation into the religion. This is a way in which it affirms the confidence that the "spiritual work" of the priest in question is done "correctly." That is to say, that initiation alone does not qualify one to practice, which is why training must be undergone (that implies collective ritual practices and specialized workshops) and fulfilling the requirements of the "traditional" system of HATTAF.

In general, the idea of the workshops and "trainings" is attractive for some Mexicans, a number of whom constantly say that despite what their Cuban godparents and mentors have taught them (like prayers and invocations in "Yoruba") they often do not understand the "real" meaning and nor do they pronounce them "correctly." That is because these elements and others have been transmitted orally for centuries, they were "lost," "distorted," or "altered."

Chief Atanda had a policy of "respecting" that the members and participants apply their "own system" of ritual practice on a private and individual level – in the case most were *santeros* – but on a public and collective level, the HATTAF system had to be used, at least for those who wanted to belong to the organization. However, in fact, these boundaries were ambiguous and appeared to cause confusion. A number of the members of the association even began to make distinction between "the Cuban" and "the African" ways of doing things. Some Mexicans had their basic religious objects "calibrated," that is, to the material representations of their deities (stones, seeds, etc.) received from the hands of Cuban priests, elements supposedly "essential" to the Yoruba religious tradition but not customarily used in Cuba, were added. For some Mexicans, this calibration meant "completing" these *objects*. As is to be expected, this was frowned on by some Cubans as it cast doubt on their own model of "tradition" and religious practice.

Finally, the initial enthusiasm was marred by various factors: the language barrier that often limited communication, misunderstandings and "gossip" on money matters, conflicts around leadership and official appointments, the geographical distance that was an obstacle to the continuity of the "teaching-learning" process, and the "disillusionments" caused by the lack of reciprocity, amongst others. As for the *Ilé Ifá* Association, by February 2005 it had suspended its periodic meetings due to the lack of commitment of its members, as well as the difficulties involved in implementing "unification." Both associations appear to have suffered the same fate. Despite the expectations generated at the beginning and also the fulfillment of some aims, with time they have lost their force and the number of active members has fallen. The multiple divisions and interests observed amongst the members, subordinate the "common aims" preventing the collective "ideals" from being achieved and impeding an organized and effective micro-mobilization around them. At the same time, they reflect on a micro level what can be observed on the transnational scale, that is, the tension between orthodoxy and heterodoxy in religious praxis.

Final considerations

Since the beginning of the twentieth century, the *cabildos* (Catholic religious fraternities) from which the Afro-Cuban cults like *Santería* emerged, were transformed into socio-religious collectives in which the criterion of ethnic descent was over-taken by the criterion of religious filiation through initiation (Murphy 1993, 3, Cabrera 1996, Brown 2003, 67). But when *Santería* was trans-nationalized to other countries for example, the United States, this ethnic and racial criteria was re-activated in a complex racial context that made "the fusion of Cuban *Santería* and black nationalism" possible (Capone 1999, 305, also see Brandon 1993). This explains the opinion of the *Ilé Ifá* Association of Mexico leader when he speaks of "the racism shown by some Afro-Americans about accepting whites in the religion," as this was one of the motives for conflict between "Latino" and Afro-American practitioners in the United States.

On the contrary, in the case of Mexico, the criterion of religious filiation through initiation seems to predominate over ethnic or racial considerations. In this context, the relations between the different practitioners of *Santería* or "Yoruba religion" are not involved in broader political-racial movements, and racialized relations often take on much more subtle forms. It should also be said that the creation of formalized networks in associations or groups today, offer the possibility of insertion in an African lineage, through membership that does not necessarily imply ritual kinship established through initiation or blood ties. It appears to be increasingly common that belonging to an association or an organization that is legally established, or at least "recognized," has become a form of symbolic capital that "supports status" and defends a "religious model" always argued to be "traditional" and thus the true one. This is an aspect that can be observed not only at a more local level but articulated and often fundamentally encouraged on a transnational scale.

Thus, "Re-Africanization," as a number of authors have already indicated, does not mean wanting to be African or claim African ethnic origin, but rather become intellectualized by learning about Yoruba culture, considered to be the matrix of different forms of Afro-American religions – as is the case of *Santería* (Capone 1999, Frigerio 2004). The leaders of Re-Africanization in Mexico identify themselves as "Yoruba" or "Yoruba-descendants" in a religious or "spiritual" sense rather than ethnically or racially.

It should also be mentioned that this trend towards Re-Africanization is not the same as *wiping the slate clean* with respect to the previous religious and spiritual path of the devotees within this movement. In the individual sphere, what we can observe instead is an appropriation that does not replace one tradition with another but which enriches and complements it, incorporating new elements that respond to the personal needs, interpretations, interests and worries of the followers. In the terrain of religious praxis, Re-Africanization generates ritual innovations that are now based not only on the experience and knowledge transmitted orally by the elders of the religion, but also "theoretically" and in practical terms from the own research and experience of the initiate, a process in which communication technologies and transnational networks play an unavoidable part.

Notes

1. Translated by Susan Jones Harris.

2. During its evolution in Cuba, *Santería* had incorporated elements from Catholicism as well as Kardecian spiritualism. To this we should add its ritual articulation with other cults of African origin. Kali Argyriadis points out that in the case of Cuba this set of complementary forms is included within the generic term of *The Religion* (1999). In this article I shall use the term "*Santería*" to refer to this original complementary universe as despite the debate surrounding it, in Mexico it is still used as a generic category. More recently the denomination "Yoruba Religion" has become increasingly popular.

3. The consultant is the subject whose only interest is in making or maintaining contact with *Santería*, at least to start with, who

solicits the services offered by its priests, particularly in relation to methods of divining and the "works" derived from them ("cleansing", "tasks" ...)

4. For the case of Guadalajara see Esparza, 2002; for the case of Veracruz see Argyriadis, 2008.

5. Roughly speaking it can be said that the first contacts between outsiders and initiates (or specialists) were generally established through what is commonly called *"registro"* or "consultation" that consists of using different divining techniques (oracles). By means of these oracles, the initiates facilitate the communication with the deities of their devotion, generally called *orishas* or saints, considered to be the intermediaries between Olodumare/Olofin (the creator, God) and men. Each Santero is the son of a particular *orisha* that is ritually and symbolically crowned on his head during the initiation ceremony called "coronation of the saint" or "making a saint"). The type and complexity of the oracles used by the initiates will depend on their hierarchy. Usually they use the coconut, the cowrie shells and the oracle of Ifá, this last one being the exclusive province of the *babawalos*, who have gone through a special initiation ceremony generally reserved for heterosexual men.

6. *Resguardos* are objects ritually prepared for those who possess them "to protect against or drive away misfortune". Some of them, like necklaces and warriors are considered to be part of the levels of initiation, although of "minor level" compared to the central ceremony of initiation "crowned of the saint or consecration of Ifá.

7. The basis of the *Santería's* social organization is the house or *Ilé*, made up by a set of people who through ritual kinship ties form a religious family or saint's house. The godfather or godmother become the symbolic father or mother of the godchildren they initiate. And the godchildren of a one particular godfather or godmother become "brothers of the saint". This ritual ties extends to earlier generations that connect them to a more extended genealogical "branch".

8. *Santeros* in the north of Mexico were accused of having ties with drug traffickers and of carrying out ritual human sacrifices.

9. Today the presence of *Santería* goes from the communications media, markets, esoteric centers, private temples to musical events and cultural festivals.

10. The *babalawo* generally tends to be considered at the top of the hierarchical organization of *Santería*. This priest dominates the divination method called the oracle of *Ifá* (considered to be the most complex).

11. The Mexicans themselves are not at all exempt from accusations related to "robbery" and "cheating", not only by their fellow nationals but also by the Cubans. To this we should add accusations that the Mexicans, especially "the *chilangos*" – people from Mexico City – make "a botched job of things" and do not work according to "tradition".

12. Interview with María M., Mexico, D.F., 11 February, 2004.

13. With respect to the categories on "black identity" in Mexico, Odile Hoffmann underlines that the term Afro-Mexican or Afro-Mexicanist "begins to have some degree of consensus in Mexico, in the same way as it has imposed itself in other Latin American countries (Afro-Colombian, Afro-Brazilian etcetera)". Although she also says that "neither official discourse nor influential political figures at national level use any particular type of categorization to refer to populations that identify themselves as 'dark-skinned' (*morenos*) or 'Afro-mestizos'" (2006, 106-107).

14. One of his main sources of information was the work of Aguirre Beltrán, – the father of "Afro-Mexican" studies – thanks to which, according to him, "I was able to learn about the history of the black in my country, Mexico."

15. HATTAF is the acronym for *"Healing, Teaching and Tourism Temple of African Faith International"*

16. He refers metaphorically to his Cuban wife.

17. Amongst other things, this *babalawo* points out that "[...] The tradition related with Africa has died out amongst the blacks of Mexico's Pacific coast. But that is not the same for their contribution to the Mexican's genetic composition." M.E.C., "Las Religiones Afrocubanas en México", paper presented at the *IV Coloquio Internacional de Religión y Sociedad: Religiones Afroamericanas y las identidades en un mundo globalizado*, Havana, Cuba, July 2005.

18. The first of these was held in Ile Ife, Nigeria in 1981 and the last of the nine held up until now, in Brazil. For more details see Capone (2005)

19. Lagos and Osogbo, Nigeria; London, United Kingdom; Sacramento, California; Key West and Orlando, Florida and now in the metropolitan area of Mexico City.

20. *Oriaté* is a master of the central ceremony of initiation into Santería

21. It was through this Temple that a group of Mexicans, including one woman, went to Nigeria to be initiated into Ifá. This was an event that caused debate, as this ritual arena has, for many years, been predominantly male.

Bibliography

Aguirre Beltrán, Gonzalo. 1989[1946]. *La población negra de México: estudio etnohistórico.* México: FCE/UV/INI/Gobierno del Estado de Veracruz.

Argyriadis, Kali. 1999. *La religión à la Havane. Actualité des répresentations et des pratiques cultuelles havanaises.* Paris: Éditions des archives contemporaines, Centre d'anthropologie des mondes contemporains, EHESS.

Argyriadis, Kali. 2000. Des Noirs sorciers aux babalaos: analyse du paradoxe du rapport à l'Afrique à La Havane. *Cahier d'Études africaines* XL(4) 160: 649-674.

Argyriadis, Kali. 2005. El desarrollo del turismo religiosos en La Habana y la acusación de mercantilismo. *Desacatos* 18: 29-52, Mayo-Agosto.

Argyriadis, Kali. 2006. Les bata deux fois sacres : la construction de la tradition musicale et chorégraphique afro-cubaine. *Civilisations* LII (1-2): 45-74.

Argyriadis, Kali. 2008. *Repertorio afrocubano y artistas promotres de la cultura "afro" en México: del espacio local (Veracruz) a la red transnacional.* Ponencia presentada en el Congreso Diáspora, Nación y Diferencia. Poblaciones de origen africano en México y Centroamérica, Veracruz, Ver., Junio.

Argyriadis, Kali y Stefania Capone. 2004. Cubanía et *santería*: les enjeux politiques de la transnationalisation religieuse. *Civilisations* LI (1-2): 81-137.

Argyriadis, Kali y Nahayeilli Juárez Huet. 2006. *Santería y Africanía. Procesos de relocalización en la Ciudad de México y el Puerto de Veracruz.* Ponencia presentada en las Jornadas de estudio del grupo de investigación sobre Translocalización y relocalización de lo religioso. México, D.F., *Idymov* (CIESAS/IRD/ICANH), 16 de Mayo.

Basch, Linda, Nina Glick Schiller and Cristina Blanc Szanton. 1994. *Nations Unbound. Transnational Projects, Postcolonial Predicaments and Deterritorialized Nation-States*. Gordon and Breach Publishers.

Brandon, George. 1993. *Santería from Africa to the new World: the dead sell memories*. Bloomington: Indiana University Press.

Brown, David. 2003. *Santería enthroned: art, ritual, and innovation in an afro-cuban religion*. Chicago: University of Chicago.

Cabrera, Lydia. 1996[1954]. *El monte*. La Habana : Editorial SI-MAR.

Capone, Stefania. 1999. *La quête de l'Afrique dans le candomblé. Pouvoir et tradition au Brésil*. París: Karthala.

Capone, Stefania. 2000. Entre Yoruba et Bantu : l'influence des stéréotypes raciaux dans les études afro-américaines. *Cahiers d'études africaines* 157 (XV-1): 55-77.

Capone, Stefania. 2004. A propos des notions de globalisation et de transnationalisation. *Civilisations* LI (1-2): 9-21.

Capone, Stefania. 2005. *Les Yoruba du Nouveau Monde. Religion, ethnicité et nationalisme noir aux Etats-Unis*. Paris: Karthala.

Esparza, Juan Carlos. 2002. El sistema Ocha-Ifá, producto de importación garantizado. In *Cambios religiosos globales y reacomodos locales. Altexto 41-75* coord. Karla Y. Covarrubias y Rogelio de la Mora. México: Colima.

Frigerio, Alejandro. 2004. Re-Africanization in Secondary Religious Diasporas: Constructing a World Religion. *Civilisations* LI (1-2): 39-60.

Glick Schiller Nina and Georges E. Fouron. 1999. Terrains of blood and nation: Haitian Transnacional social fields. *Ethnic and Racial Studies* 22: 341-366.

Gutiérrez Zúñiga, Cristina. 2008. La danza neo-tradicional como oferta espiritual en la estantería exotérica new-age. In *Raíces en movimiento. Prácticas religiosas tradicionales en contextos translocales* coord. Alejandra Aguilar, Kali Argyriadis, Renée De La Torre, Cristina Gutiérrez. Guadalajara: El Colegio de Jalisco / IRD / CEMCA / CIESAS / ITESO.

Hagedorn, Catherine J. 2001. *Divine Utterances: The performance of afro-cuban santería*. Washington/Londres: Smithsonian Institution Press.

Hoffmann, Odile. 2006. Negros y afromestizos en México: viejas y nuevas lecturas de un mundo olvidado. *Revista Mexicana de Sociología*, año 68, 1: 103-135.

Juárez Huet Nahayeilli Beatriz. 2004. La *santería* dans la ville de Mexico: ébauche etnographique. *Civilisations* LI (1-2): 61-79.

Juárez Huet Nahayeilli Beatriz. 2007. *Un pedacito de Dios en casa: transnacionalización, relocalización y práctica de la santería en la ciudad de México*. Tesis de doctorado, El Colegio de Michoacán.

Knauer, Lisa Maya. 2001. Afrocubanidad translocal: la rumba y la *santería* en Nueva York y La Habana. In *Culturas encontradas: Cuba y los Estados Unidos* coord. Rafael Hernández y John H. Coastworth. La Habana: CIDCC Juan Marinelo, DRCLAS Universidad de Harvard: 11-31.

Lomnitz, Claudio. 1994. *Las salidas del laberinto. Cultura e ideología en el espacio nacional mexicano*. México: Joaquín Mortiz.

Martínez Furé, Rogelio. 1979. *Diálogos imaginarios*, La Habana, Cuba: Editorial Arte y Literatura.

Martínez Montiel, Luz María, 1995, (coord.) *Presencia Africana en México*. México: CNCA.

Matory, James Lorand. 1998. Trasatlántica, 1830-1950. *Horizontes Antropológicos* año 4 (9): 263-292.

Matory, James Lorand. 2001. El nuevo imperio yoruba: textos, migración y el auge transatlántico de la nación lucumí. In *Culturas encontradas: Cuba y los Estados Unidos* coord. Rafael Hernández y John H. Coastworth. La Habana: CIDCC Juan Marinelo, DRCLAS Universidad de Harvard: 167-188.

Menéndez, Lázara. 2002. *Rodar el coco. Proceso de cambio en la santería*. La Habana, Cuba: Editorial de Ciencias Sociales.

Moore, Robin. 2001-2002. La fiebre de la rumba. *Encuentro de la Cultura Cubana* 23: 175-194.

Murphy, Joseph. 1993 [1988]. *Santería, African spirits in América*. Boston: Bascon Press.

Orotiz, Fernando. 2001 [1906]. *Los Negros Brujos*. La Habana, Cuba: Editorial de Ciencias Sociales, 1ª reimpresión.

Peel, J. D. Y. 2000. *Religious Encounters and the making of the Yoruba*. Bloomington, Indianapolis: Indiana University Press.

Prandi, Reginaldo. 1998. Referêrencias sociais das religiões afro-brasileiras: sincretismo, branqueamento, africanização. *Horizontes Antropológicos*, año 4, 8: 151-167.

Wade, Peter. 1997. *Gente negra, Nación mestiza. Dinámicas de las identidades raciales en Colombia*. Bogotá: Uniantoquia/ICAN/ Siglo del Hombre/Uniandes.

Notes on Contributors

Carlos AGUDELO is a sociologist, researcher of CEMCA, Center of Mexican and Central American Studies. His research topics multiculturalism, identities, citizenship and political action in black populations in Latin America. He has worked in Colombia and Central America. Some publications: Politique et populations noires en Colombie. Enjeux du multiculturalismo (L'Harmattan., Paris, 2004), *Retos del multiculturalismo en Colombia. Política y poblaciones negras* (La Carreta, Medellín, 2005), whit Capucine Boidin and Livio Sansone (coord.), *Autour de l'Atlantique noir » Une polyphonie de perspectivas* (IHEAL, Paris 2009),

Elisabeth CUNIN is sociologist at the Institut de Recherche pour le Développement (IRD-France) and at present associate researcher at the University of Quintana Roo and CIESAS (Centro de Investigación y Estudios Superiores en Antropología Social) in Mexico. Her research deals with social construction of ethnic and racial categories in the case of afrodescendant population in Colombia, Mexico and Belize. Her most recent publications: edition of *Textos en diáspora. Una antología sobre afrodescendientes en las Américas* (México, INAH-CEMCA-IFEA-IRD, 2008); and of *Mestizaje, diferencia y nación. "Lo negro" en América Central y el Caribe* (México, INAH-UNAM-CEMCA-IRD, colección Africanía, 2010).

Miguel GONZALEZ holds a PhD in Political Science (York University, 2008). His research focuses on indigenous social movements, territorial autonomy regimes, and sub-national governance. He co-authored (with Pierre Frühling and Hans Peter-Buvollen) Etnicidad y Nación. El Desarrollo de la Autonomía de la Costa Atlántica de Nicaragua. 1987-2007, Guatemala: F&G Editores, 2007), and is co-editor of The Rama: Struggling for Land and Culture, Nicaragua: URACCAN & University of Tromso-Norway, 2006. Currently, he teaches in the International Development Studies Program at York University in Toronto, Canada.

Odile HOFFMANN is geographer at the Institut de Recherche pour le Développement (IRD-France) and at present member of the research group Migrations and Society (URMIS), at the University Paris Diderot. Formerly Director of CEMCA, french Center for Mexican and Centramerican Studies, in Mexico. Her research deals with afrodescendant population in Colombia, Mexico and Belize, particularly their spatial and territorial dynamics. Her most recent publications: edition of *Política e identidad, afrodescendientes en México y América* Central (México, INAH-UNAM-CEMCA-IRD, colección Africanía, 2010). And, with Ch.Poiret and C.Audebert, the edition of the Journal REMI issue of 2011 (27) " La construction de l'altérité dans l'espace noir atlantique". (www.odilehoffmann.com)

Nahayeilli B. JUÁREZ HUET received her Ph.D. in Social Anthropology from *El Colegio de Michoacán*, in 2007. The topic of her research is the transnationalization and relocation of Cuban Santeria in Mexico City and the Yucatan Peninsula. She is currently a research fellow at the Center for Research and Advanced Studies in Social Anthropology (CIESAS) venue: Mérida, Yucatán. She is also a member of two main researcher's network. The former, dedicated to the study of Afro-American religions and its transnationalization and relocation in Mexico; the second is organized around a project named AFRODESC: "People of African descent and slaveries: domination, identification and heritages in the Americas 15th - 21st centuries".

Gloria LARA MILLAN is a professor-researcher in Department of History at Universidad Michoacana de San Nicolás Hidalgo, Mexico. Collaborates in civil and community organizations and participates in Community Development Projects. In academic work focuses on reflection on the exercise of citizenship, political participation, identity and political mobilization of African descent populations in the coast of Oaxaca, Mexico. Recent publications: "Les dimensions ethnique et raciale dans la construction politique d'un sujet« afro » ou « noir » au Mexique", Revue européenne des Migrations Internationales", (27) 1, 2011, pp. 89-106 ; Coordinadora del libro Experiencias y resultados de la acción afirmativa en Latinoamerica, ANUIES-BM, 2011.

Christian RINAUDO is Professor in the Department of Sociology at Nice-Sophia Antipolis University (France), and member of the research group Migrations and Society (URMIS). His research deals with the ethnic boundaries and categorizations in French and Latin America urban contexts. His most recent publications : Afro-mestizaje y fronteras étnicas. Una mirada desde el Puerto de Veracruz (Veracruz: Editorial de la Universidad Veracruzana-IRD-AFRODESC, 2011). He has also edited (with F. Ávila Domínguez and R. Pérez Montfort) the volume Circulaciones culturales. Lo afrocaribeño entre Cartagena, Veracruz, y La Habana (México D.F.: CIESAS-IRD-Universidad de Cartagena-AFRODESC, 2011).

$\mathcal{I}ndex$

United Black Association for
Development 42
US-AID (United States
Agency for International
Development) 70

Veracruz 89, 90, 97-99, 120,
139, 140, 143-159, 165

witchcraft 168, 171
World Bank 64-66, 74, 121

YATAMA (Yapti Tasba
Masrika Nanih Asla
Takanka-The Organization
of The Peoples of Mother
Earth) 9-14, 17, 19, 20
Yoruba, Yoruba religion,
Yoruba-descendents 167,
170-173, 176-183